JUNIOR GREAT BOOKS

SERIES 4

BOOK ONE

◆ ◆ ◆

The interpretive discussion program that moves students toward excellence in reading comprehension, critical thinking, and writing

JUNIOR GREAT BOOKS®

SERIES 4

BOOK ONE

THE GREAT BOOKS FOUNDATION

A nonprofit educational organization

ISBN 978-1-933147-04-8

15 14 13 12 11 10

Printed in the United States of America

Published and distributed by

THE GREAT BOOKS FOUNDATION
A nonprofit educational organization

35 East Wacker Drive, Suite 400

Chicago, IL 60601

CONTENTS

It was about eleven o'clock at night.

Thank You, M'am

Langston Hughes

She was a large woman with a large purse that had everything in it but a hammer and nails. It had a long strap, and she carried it slung across her shoulder. It was about eleven o'clock at night, dark, and she was walking alone, when a boy ran up behind her and tried to snatch her purse. The strap broke with the sudden single tug the boy gave it from behind. But the boy's weight and the weight of the purse combined caused him to lose his balance. Instead of taking off full blast as he had hoped, the boy fell on his back on the sidewalk and his legs flew up. The large woman simply turned around and kicked him right square in his blue-jeaned sitter. Then she reached down, picked the boy up by his shirt front, and shook him until his teeth rattled.

After that the woman said, "Pick up my pocketbook, boy, and give it here."

She still held him tightly. But she bent down enough to permit him to stoop and pick up her purse. Then she said, "Now ain't you ashamed of yourself?"

Firmly gripped by his shirt front, the boy said, "Yes'm."

The woman said, "What did you want to do it for?"

The boy said, "I didn't aim to."

She said, "You a lie!"

By that time two or three people passed, stopped, turned to look, and some stood watching.

"If I turn you loose, will you run?" asked the woman.

"Yes'm," said the boy.

"Then I won't turn you loose," said the woman. She did not release him.

"Lady, I'm sorry," whispered the boy.

"Um-hum! Your face is dirty. I got a great mind to wash your face for you. Ain't you got nobody home to tell you to wash your face?"

"No'm," said the boy.

"Then it will get washed this evening," said the large woman, starting up the street, dragging the frightened boy behind her.

He looked as if he were fourteen or fifteen, frail and willow-wild, in tennis shoes and blue jeans.

The woman said, "You ought to be my son. I would teach you right from wrong. Least I can do right now is to wash your face. Are you hungry?"

"No'm," said the being-dragged boy. "I just want you to turn me loose."

"Was I bothering *you* when I turned that corner?" asked the woman.

"No'm."

"But you put yourself in contact with *me*," said the woman. "If you think that that contact is not going to last awhile, you got another thought coming. When I get through with you, sir, you are going to remember Mrs. Luella Bates Washington Jones."

Sweat popped out on the boy's face and he began to struggle. Mrs. Jones stopped, jerked him around in front of her, put a half nelson about his neck, and continued to drag him up the street. When she got to her door, she dragged the boy inside, down a hall, and into a large kitchenette-furnished room at the rear of the house. She switched on the light and left the door open. The boy could hear other roomers laughing and talking in the large house. Some of their doors were open, too, so he knew he and the woman were not alone. The woman still had him by the neck in the middle of her room.

She said, "What is your name?"

"Roger," answered the boy.

"Then, Roger, you go to that sink and wash your face," said the woman, whereupon she turned him loose—at last. Roger looked at the door—looked at the woman—looked at the door—*and went to the sink.*

"Let the water run until it gets warm," she said. "Here's a clean towel."

"You gonna take me to jail?" asked the boy, bending over the sink.

"Not with that face, I would not take you nowhere," said the woman. "Here I am trying to get home to cook me a bite to eat, and you snatch my pocketbook! Maybe you ain't been to your supper either, late as it be. Have you?"

"There's nobody home at my house," said the boy.

"Then we'll eat," said the woman. "I believe you're hungry—or been hungry—to try to snatch my pocketbook!"

"I want a pair of blue suede shoes," said the boy.

"Well, you didn't have to snatch *my* pocketbook to get some suede shoes," said Mrs. Luella Bates Washington Jones. "You could of asked me."

"M'am?"

The water dripping from his face, the boy looked at her. There was a long pause. A very long pause. After he had dried his face and not knowing what else to do, dried it again, the boy turned around, wondering what next. The door was open. He could make a dash for it down the hall. He could run, run, run, *run*!

The woman was sitting on the daybed. After a while she said, "I were young once and I wanted things I could not get."

There was another long pause. The boy's mouth opened. Then he frowned, not knowing he frowned.

The woman said, "Um-hum! You thought I was going to say *but*, didn't you? You thought I was going to say, *but I didn't snatch people's pocketbooks.* Well, I wasn't going to say that." Pause. Silence. "I have done things, too, which I would not tell you, son—neither tell God, if he didn't already know. Everybody's got something in common. So you set down while I fix us something to eat. You might run that comb through your hair so you will look presentable."

In another corner of the room behind a screen was a gas plate and an icebox. Mrs. Jones got up and went behind the screen. The woman did not watch the boy to see if he was going to run now, nor did she watch her purse, which she left behind her on the daybed. But the boy took care to sit on the far side of the room, away from the purse, where he thought she could easily see him out of the corner of her eye if she wanted to. He did not trust the woman *not* to trust him. And he did not want to be mistrusted now.

"Do you need somebody to go to the store," asked the boy, "maybe to get some milk or something?"

"Don't believe I do," said the woman, "unless you just want sweet milk yourself. I was going to make cocoa out of this canned milk I got here."

"That will be fine," said the boy.

She heated some lima beans and ham she had in the icebox, made the cocoa, and set the table. The woman did not ask the boy anything about where he lived, or his folks, or anything else that would embarrass him. Instead, as they ate, she told him about her job in a hotel beauty shop that stayed open late, what the work was like, and how all kinds of women came in and out, blondes, redheads, and Spanish. Then she cut him a half of her ten-cent cake.

"Eat some more, son," she said.

When they were finished eating, she got up and said, "Now here, take this ten dollars and buy yourself some blue suede shoes. And next time, do not make the mistake of latching onto *my* pocketbook *nor nobody else's*—because shoes got by devilish ways will burn your feet. I got to get my rest now. But from here on in, son, I hope you will behave yourself."

She led him down the hall to the front door and opened it. "Good night! Behave yourself, boy!" she said, looking out into the street as he went down the steps.

The boy wanted to say something other than, "Thank you, m'am," to Mrs. Luella Bates Washington Jones, but although his lips moved, he couldn't even say that as he turned at the foot of the barren stoop and looked up at the large woman in the door. Then she shut the door.

What was that shining in the old woman's hand?

THE GOLD COIN

Alma Flor Ada

Juan had been a thief for many years. Because he did his stealing by night, his skin had become pale and sickly. Because he spent his time either hiding or sneaking about, his body had become shriveled and bent. And because he had neither friend nor relative to make him smile, his face was always twisted into an angry frown.

One night, drawn by a light shining through the trees, Juan came upon a hut. He crept up to the door and through a crack saw an old woman sitting at a plain wooden table.

What was that shining in her hand? Juan wondered. He could not believe his eyes: It was a gold coin. Then he heard the woman say to herself, "I must be the richest person in the world."

Juan decided instantly that all the woman's gold must be his. He thought that the easiest thing to do was to watch until the woman left. Juan hid in the bushes and huddled under his poncho, waiting for the right moment to enter the hut.

Juan was half asleep when he heard knocking at the door and the sound of insistent voices. A few minutes later, he saw the woman, wrapped in a black cloak, leave the hut with two men at her side.

Here's my chance! Juan thought. And, forcing open a window, he climbed into the empty hut.

He looked about eagerly for the gold. He looked under the bed. It wasn't there. He looked in the cupboard. It wasn't there, either. Where could it be? Close to despair, Juan tore away some beams supporting the thatch roof.

Finally, he gave up. There was simply no gold in the hut.

All I can do, he thought, is find the old woman and make her tell me where she's hidden it.

So he set out along the path that she and her two companions had taken.

It was daylight by the time Juan reached the river. The countryside had been deserted, but here, along the riverbank, were two huts. Nearby, a man and his son were hard at work, hoeing potatoes.

It had been a long, long time since Juan had spoken to another human being. Yet his desire to find the woman was so strong that he went up to the farmers and asked, in a hoarse, raspy voice, "Have you seen a short, gray-haired woman, wearing a black cloak?"

"Oh, you must be looking for Doña Josefa," the young boy said. "Yes, we've seen her. We went to fetch her this morning, because my grandfather had another attack of—"

"Where is she now?" Juan broke in.

"She is long gone," said the father with a smile. "Some people from across the river came looking for her, because someone in their family is sick."

"How can I get across the river?" Juan asked anxiously.

"Only by boat," the boy answered. "We'll row you across later, if you'd like." Then turning back to his work, he added, "But first we must finish digging up the potatoes."

The thief muttered, "Thanks." But he quickly grew impatient. He grabbed a hoe and began to help the pair of farmers. The sooner we finish, the sooner we'll get across the river, he thought. And the sooner I'll get to my gold!

It was dusk when they finally laid down their hoes. The soil had been turned, and the wicker baskets were brimming with potatoes.

"Now can you row me across?" Juan asked the father anxiously.

"Certainly," the man said. "But let's eat supper first!"

Juan had forgotten the taste of a home-cooked meal, and the pleasure that comes from sharing it with others. As he sopped up the last of the stew with a chunk of dark bread, memories of other meals came back to him from far away and long ago.

By the light of the moon, father and son guided their boat across the river.

"What a wonderful healer Doña Josefa is!" the boy told Juan. "All she had to do to make Abuelo better was give him a cup of her special tea."

"Yes, and not only that," his father added, "she brought him a gold coin."

Juan was stunned. It was one thing for Doña Josefa to go around helping people, but how could she go around handing out gold coins—*his gold coins*?

When the threesome finally reached the other side of the river, they saw a young man sitting outside his hut.

"This fellow is looking for Doña Josefa," the father said, pointing to Juan.

"Oh, she left some time ago," the young man said.

"Where to?" Juan asked tensely.

"Over to the other side of the mountain," the young man replied, pointing to the vague outline of mountains in the night sky.

"How did she get there?" Juan asked, trying to hide his impatience.

"By horse," the young man answered. "They came on horseback to get her because someone had broken his leg."

"Well, then I need a horse, too," Juan said urgently.

"Tomorrow," the young man replied softly. "Perhaps I can take you tomorrow, maybe the next day. First I must finish harvesting the corn."

So Juan spent the next day in the fields, bathed in sweat from sunup to sundown.

Yet each ear of corn that he picked seemed to bring him closer to his treasure. And later that evening, when he helped the young man husk several ears so they could boil them for supper, the yellow kernels glittered like gold coins.

While they were eating, Juan thought about Doña Josefa. Why, he wondered, would someone who said she was the world's richest woman spend her time taking care of every sick person for miles around?

The following day, the two set off at dawn. Juan could not recall when he last had noticed the beauty of the sunrise. He felt strangely moved by the sight of the mountains, barely lit by the faint rays of the morning sun.

As they neared the foothills, the young man said, "I'm not surprised you're looking for Doña Josefa. The whole countryside needs her. I went for her because my wife had been running a high fever. In no time at all Doña Josefa had her on the road to recovery. And what's more, my friend, she brought her a gold coin!"

Juan groaned inwardly. To think that someone could hand out gold so freely! What a strange woman Doña

Josefa is, Juan thought. Not only is she willing to help one person after another, but she doesn't mind traveling all over the countryside to do it!

"Well, my friend," said the young man finally, "this is where I must leave you. But you don't have far to walk. See that house over there? It belongs to the man who broke his leg."

The young man stretched out his hand to say goodbye. Juan stared at it for a moment. It had been a long, long time since the thief had shaken hands with anyone. Slowly, he pulled out a hand from under his poncho. When his companion grasped it firmly in his own, Juan felt suddenly warmed, as if by the rays of the sun.

But after he thanked the young man, Juan ran down the road. He was still eager to catch up with Doña Josefa. When he reached the house, a woman and a child were stepping down from a wagon.

"Have you seen Doña Josefa?" Juan asked.

"We've just taken her to Don Teodosio's," the woman said. "His wife is sick, you know—"

"How do I get there?" Juan broke in. "I've got to see her."

"It's too far to walk," the woman said amiably. "If you'd like, I'll take you there tomorrow. But first I must gather my squash and beans."

So Juan spent yet another long day in the fields. Working beneath the summer sun, Juan noticed that his skin had begun to tan. And although he had to stoop down to pick the squash, he found that he could now stretch his body. His back had begun to straighten, too.

Later, when the little girl took him by the hand to show him a family of rabbits burrowed under a fallen tree, Juan's face broke into a smile. It had been a long, long time since Juan had smiled.

Yet his thoughts kept coming back to the gold.

The following day, the wagon carrying Juan and the woman lumbered along a road lined with coffee fields.

The woman said, "I don't know what we would have done without Doña Josefa. I sent my daughter to our neighbor's house, who then brought Doña Josefa on horseback. She set my husband's leg and then showed me how to brew a special tea to lessen the pain."

Getting no reply, she went on. "And, as if that weren't enough, she brought him a gold coin. Can you imagine such a thing?"

Juan could only sigh. No doubt about it, he thought, Doña Josefa is someone special. But Juan didn't know whether to be happy that Doña Josefa had so much gold she could freely hand it out, or angry for her having already given so much of it away.

When they finally reached Don Teodosio's house, Doña Josefa was already gone. But here, too, there was work that needed to be done. . . .

Juan stayed to help with the coffee harvest. As he picked the red berries, he gazed up from time to time at the trees that grew, row upon row, along the hillsides. What a calm, peaceful place this is, he thought.

The next morning, Juan was up at daybreak. Bathed in the soft dawn light, the mountains seemed to smile at him. When Don Teodosio offered him a lift on horseback, Juan found it difficult to have to say goodbye.

"What a good woman Doña Josefa is!" Don Teodosio said, as they rode down the hill toward the sugar cane fields. "The minute she heard about my wife being sick, she came with her special herbs. And as if that weren't enough, she brought my wife a gold coin!"

In the stifling heat, the kind that often signals the approach of a storm, Juan simply sighed and mopped his brow. The pair continued riding for several hours in silence.

Juan then realized he was back in familiar territory, for they were now on the stretch of road he had traveled only a week ago—though how much longer it now seemed to him. He jumped off Don Teodosio's horse and broke into a run.

This time the gold would not escape him! But he had to move quickly, so he could find shelter before the storm broke.

Out of breath, Juan finally reached Doña Josefa's hut. She was standing by the door, shaking her head slowly as she surveyed the ransacked house.

"So I've caught up with you at last!" Juan shouted, startling the old woman. "Where's the gold?"

"The gold coin?" Doña Josefa said, surprised and looking at Juan intently. "Have you come for the gold coin? I've been trying hard to give it to someone who might need it," Doña Josefa said. "First to an old man who had just gotten over a bad attack. Then to a young woman who had been running a fever. Then to a man with a broken leg. And finally to Don Teodosio's wife. But none of them would take it. They all said, 'Keep it. There must be someone who needs it more.'"

Juan did not say a word.

"You must be the one who needs it," Doña Josefa said.

She took the coin out of her pocket and handed it to him. Juan stared at the coin, speechless.

At that moment a young girl appeared, her long braid bouncing as she ran. "Hurry, Doña Josefa, please!" she said breathlessly. "My mother is all alone, and the baby is due any minute."

"Of course, dear," Doña Josefa replied. But as she glanced up at the sky, she saw nothing but black clouds. The storm was nearly upon them. Doña Josefa sighed deeply.

"But how can I leave now? Look at my house! I don't know what has happened to the roof. The storm will wash the whole place away!"

And there was a deep sadness in her voice.

Juan took in the child's frightened eyes, Doña Josefa's sad, distressed face, and the ransacked hut.

"Go ahead, Doña Josefa," he said. "Don't worry about your house. I'll see that the roof is back in shape, good as new."

The woman nodded gratefully, drew her cloak about her shoulders, and took the child by the hand. As she turned to leave, Juan held out his hand. "Here, take this," he said, giving her the gold coin. "I'm sure the newborn will need it more than I."

My mother sang as she combed my hair.

TUESDAY OF THE OTHER JUNE

Norma Fox Mazer

"Be good, be good, be good, be good, my Junie," my mother sang as she combed my hair—a song, a story, a croon, a plea. "It's just you and me, two women alone in the world, June darling of my heart. We have enough troubles getting by, we surely don't need a single one more, so you keep your sweet self out of fighting and all that bad stuff. People can be little hearted, but turn the other cheek, smile at the world, and the world'll surely smile back."

We stood in front of the mirror as she combed my hair, combed and brushed and smoothed. Her head came just above mine; she said when I grew another inch she'd stand on a stool to brush my hair. "I'm not giving up this pleasure!" And she laughed her long honey laugh.

My mother was April, my grandmother had been May, I was June. "And someday," said my mother, "you'll have a daughter of your own. What will you name her?"

"January!" I'd yell when I was little. "February! No, November!" My mother laughed her honey laugh. She had little emerald eyes that warmed me like the sun.

Every day when I went to school, she went to work. "Sometimes I stop what I'm doing," she said, "lay down my tools, and stop everything, because all I can think about is you. Wondering what you're doing and if you need me. Now, Junie, if anyone ever bothers you—"

"—I walk away, run away, come on home as fast as my feet will take me," I recited.

"Yes. You come to me. You just bring me your trouble, because I'm here on this earth to love you and take care of you."

I was safe with her. Still, sometimes I woke up at night and heard footsteps slowly creeping up the stairs. It wasn't my mother—she was asleep in the bed across the room—so it was robbers, thieves, and murderers, creeping slowly . . . slowly . . . slowly toward my bed.

I stuffed my hand into my mouth. If I screamed and woke her, she'd be tired at work tomorrow. The robbers and thieves filled the warm darkness and slipped across the floor more quietly than cats. Rigid under the covers, I stared at the shifting dark and bit my knuckles and never knew when I fell asleep again.

In the morning we sang in the kitchen. "Bill Grogan's GOAT! Was feelin' FINE! Ate three red shirts, right off the

LINE!" I made sandwiches for our lunches, she made pancakes for breakfast, but all she ate was one pancake and a cup of coffee. "Gotta fly, can't be late."

I wanted to be rich and take care of her. She worked too hard; her pretty hair had gray in it that she joked about. "Someday," I said, "I'll buy you a real house, and you'll never work in a pot factory again."

"Such delicious plans," she said. She checked the windows to see if they were locked. "Do you have your key?"

I lifted it from the chain around my neck.

"And you'll come right home from school and—"

"—I won't light fires or let strangers into the house, and I won't tell anyone on the phone that I'm here alone," I finished for her.

"I know, I'm just your old worrywart mother." She kissed me twice, once on each cheek. "But you are my June, my only June, the only June."

She was wrong; there was another June. I met her when we stood next to each other at the edge of the pool the first day of swimming class in the community center.

"What's your name?" She had a deep growly voice.

"June. What's yours?"

She stared at me. "June."

"We have the same name."

"No we don't. June is *my* name, and I don't give you permission to use it. Your name is Fish Eyes." She pinched me hard. "Got it, Fish Eyes?"

The next Tuesday, the Other June again stood next to me at the edge of the pool. "What's your name?"

"June."

"Wrong. Your—name—is—Fish—Eyes."

"June."

"Fish Eyes, you are really stupid." She shoved me into the pool.

The swimming teacher looked up, frowning, from her chart. "No one in the water yet."

Later, in the locker room, I dressed quickly and wrapped my wet suit in the towel. The Other June pulled on her jeans. "You guys see that bathing suit Fish Eyes was wearing? Her mother found it in a trash can."

"She did not!"

The Other June grabbed my fingers and twisted. "Where'd she find your bathing suit?"

"She bought it; let me go."

"Poor little stupid Fish Eyes is crying. Oh, boo hoo hoo, poor little Fish Eyes."

After that, everyone called me Fish Eyes. And every Tuesday, wherever I was, there was also the Other June—at the edge of the pool, in the pool, in the locker room. In the water, she swam alongside me, blowing and huffing, knocking into me. In the locker room, she stepped on my feet, pinched my arms, hid my blouse, and knotted my braids together. She had large square teeth; she was shorter than I was, but heavier, with bigger bones and square hands. If I met her outside on the street, carrying her bathing suit and towel, she'd walk toward me, smiling a square, friendly smile. "Oh well, if it isn't Fish Eyes." Then she'd punch me, *blam*! Her whole solid weight hitting me.

I didn't know what to do about her. She was training me like a dog. After a few weeks of this, she only had to look at me, only had to growl, "I'm going to get you, Fish Eyes," for my heart to slink like a whipped dog down into my stomach. My arms were covered with bruises. When my mother noticed, I made up a story about tripping on the sidewalk.

My weeks were no longer Tuesday, Wednesday, Thursday, and so on. Tuesday was Awfulday. Wednesday was Badday. (The Tuesday bad feelings were still there.) Thursday was Betterday and Friday was Safeday. Saturday was Goodday, but Sunday was Toosoonday, and Monday—Monday was nothing but the day before Awfulday.

I tried to slow down time. Especially on the weekends, I stayed close by my mother, doing everything with her, shopping, cooking, cleaning, going to the laundromat. "Aw, sweetie, go play with your friends."

"No, I'd rather be with you." I wouldn't look at the clock or listen to the radio (they were always telling you the date and the time). I did special magic things to keep the day from going away, rapping my knuckles six times on the bathroom door six times a day and never, ever touching the chipped place on my bureau. But always I woke up to the day before Tuesday, and always, no matter how many times I circled the worn spot in the living-room rug or counted twenty-five cracks in the ceiling, Monday disappeared and once again it was Tuesday.

The Other June got bored with calling me Fish Eyes. Buffalo Brain came next, but as soon as everyone knew that, she renamed me Turkey Nose.

Now at night it wasn't robbers creeping up the stairs, but the Other June, coming to torment me. When I finally fell asleep, I dreamed of kicking her, punching, biting, pinching. In the morning, I remembered my dreams and felt brave and strong. And then I remembered all the things my mother had taught me and told me.

Be good, be good, be good, it's just us two women alone in the world . . . Oh, but if it weren't, if my father wasn't long gone, if we'd had someone else to fall back on, if my mother's mother and daddy weren't dead all these years, if my father's daddy wanted to know us instead of being glad to forget us—oh, then I would have punched the Other June with a frisky heart; I would have grabbed her arm at poolside and bitten her like the dog she had made of me.

One night, when my mother came home from work, she said, "Junie, listen to this. We're moving!"

Alaska, I thought. Florida. Arizona. Someplace far away and wonderful, someplace without the Other June.

"Wait till you hear this deal. We are going to be caretakers, troubleshooters for an eight-family apartment building. Fifty-six Blue Hill Street. Not janitors, we don't do any of the heavy work. April and June, Troubleshooters, Incorporated. If a tenant has a complaint or a problem, she comes to us, and we either take care of it or call the janitor for service. And for that little bit of work, we get to live rent free!" She swept me around in a dance. "Okay? You like it? I do!"

So. Not anywhere else, really. All the same, maybe too far to go to swimming class? "Can we move right away? Today?"

"Gimme a break, sweetie. We've got to pack, do a thousand things. I've got to line up someone with a truck to help us. Six weeks, Saturday the fifteenth." She circled it on the calendar. It was the Saturday after the last day of swimming class.

Soon, we had boxes lying everywhere, filled with clothes and towels and glasses wrapped in newspaper. Bit by bit, we cleared the rooms, leaving only what we needed right now. The dining-room table staggered on a bunched-up rug, our bureaus inched toward the front door like patient cows. On the calendar in the kitchen, my mother marked off the days until we moved, but the only days I thought about were Tuesdays—Awfuldays. Nothing else was real except the too-fast passing of time, moving toward each Tuesday . . . away from Tuesday . . . toward Tuesday. . . .

And it seemed to me that this would go on forever—that Tuesdays would come forever and I would be forever trapped by the side of the pool, the Other June whispering *Buffalo Brain Fish Eyes Turkey Nose* into my ear, while she ground her elbow into my side and smiled her square smile at the swimming teacher.

And then it ended. It was the last day of swimming class. The last Tuesday. We had all passed our tests and, as if in celebration, the Other June only pinched me twice. "And now," our swimming teacher said, "all of you are ready for the advanced class, which starts in just one month. I have a sign-up slip here. Please put your name down before you leave." Everyone but me crowded around. I went to the locker room and pulled on my clothes as fast as possible. The Other June burst through the door just as I was leaving. "Goodbye," I yelled. "Good riddance to bad trash!" Before she could pinch me again, I ran past her and then ran all the way home, singing, "Goodbye . . . goodbye . . . goodbye, good riddance to bad trash!"

Later, my mother carefully untied the blue ribbon around my swimming class diploma. "Look at this! Well, isn't this wonderful! You are on your way, you might turn into an Olympic swimmer, you never know what life will bring."

"I don't want to take more lessons."

"Oh, sweetie, it's great to be a good swimmer." But then, looking into my face, she said, "No, no, no, don't worry; you don't have to."

The next morning, I woke up hungry for the first time in weeks. No more swimming class. No more Baddays and Awfuldays. No more Tuesdays of the Other June. In the kitchen, I made hot cocoa to go with my mother's corn muffins. "It's Wednesday, Mom," I said, stirring the cocoa. "My favorite day."

"Since when?"

"Since this morning." I turned on the radio so I could hear the announcer tell the time, the temperature, and the day.

Thursday for breakfast I made cinnamon toast, Friday my mother made pancakes, and on Saturday, before we moved, we ate the last slices of bread and cleaned out the peanut butter jar.

"Some breakfast," Tilly said. "Hello, you must be June." She shook my hand. She was a friend of my mother's from work; she wore big hoop earrings, sandals, and a skirt as dazzling as a rainbow. She came in a truck with John to help us move our things.

John shouted cheerfully at me, "So you're moving." An enormous man with a face covered with little brown bumps. Was he afraid his voice wouldn't travel the distance from his mouth to my ear? "You looking at my moles?" he shouted, and he heaved our big green flowered chair down the stairs. "Don't worry, they don't bite. Ha, ha, ha!" Behind him came my mother and Tilly balancing a bureau between them, and behind them I carried a lamp and the round, flowered Mexican tray that was my mother's favorite. She had found it at a garage sale and said it was as close to foreign travel as we would ever get.

The night before, we had loaded our car, stuffing in bags and boxes until there was barely room for the two of us. But it was only when we were in the car, when we drove past Abdo's Grocery, where they always gave us credit, when I turned for a last look at our street—it was only then that I understood we were truly going to live somewhere else, in another apartment, in another place mysteriously called Blue Hill Street.

Tilly's truck followed our car.

"Oh, I'm so excited," my mother said. She laughed. "You'd think we were going across the country."

Our old car wheezed up a long, steep hill. Blue Hill Street. I looked from one side to the other, trying to see everything.

My mother drove over the crest of the hill. "And now—ta da!—our new home."

"Which house? Which one?" I looked out the window and what I saw was the Other June. She was sprawled on the stoop of a pink house, lounging back on her elbows, legs outspread, her jaws working on a wad of gum. I slid down into the seat, but it was too late. I was sure she had seen me.

My mother turned into a driveway next to a big white building with a tiny porch. She leaned on the steering wheel. "See that window there, that's our living-room window . . . and that one over there, that's your bedroom. . . ."

We went into the house, down a dim, cool hall. In our new apartment, the wooden floors clicked under our shoes, and my mother showed me everything. Her voice echoed in the empty rooms. I followed her around in a daze. Had I imagined seeing the Other June? Maybe I'd seen another girl who looked like her. A double. That could happen.

"Ho yo, where do you want this chair?" John appeared in the doorway. We brought in boxes and bags and beds and stopped only to eat pizza and drink orange juice from the carton.

"June's so quiet; do you think she'll adjust all right?" I heard Tilly say to my mother.

"Oh, definitely. She'll make a wonderful adjustment. She's just getting used to things."

But I thought that if the Other June lived on the same street as I did, I would never get used to things.

That night I slept in my own bed, with my own pillow and blanket, but with floors that creaked in strange voices and walls with cracks I didn't recognize. I didn't feel either happy or unhappy. It was as if I were waiting for something.

Monday, when the principal of Blue Hill Street School left me in Mr. Morrisey's classroom, I knew what I'd been waiting for. In that room full of strange kids, there was one person I knew. She smiled her square smile, raised her hand, and said, "She can sit next to me, Mr. Morrisey."

"Very nice of you, June M. Okay, June T, take your seat. I'll try not to get you two Junes mixed up."

I sat down next to her. She pinched my arm. "Good riddance to bad trash," she mocked.

I was back in the Tuesday swimming class only now it was worse, because every day would be Awfulday. The pinching had already started. Soon, I knew, on the playground and in the halls, kids would pass me, grinning. "Hiya, Fish Eyes."

The Other June followed me around during recess that day, droning in my ear, "You are my slave. You must do everything I say. I am your master. Say it, say, 'Yes, master, you are my master.'"

I pressed my lips together, clapped my hands over my ears, but without hope. Wasn't it only a matter of time before I said the hateful words?

"How was school?" my mother said that night.

"Okay."

She put a pile of towels in a bureau drawer. "Try not to be sad about missing your old friends, sweetie. There'll be new ones."

The next morning, the Other June was waiting for me when I left the house. "Did your mother get you that blouse in the garbage dump?" She butted me, shoving me against a tree. "Don't you speak anymore, Fish Eyes?" Grabbing my chin in her hands, she pried open my mouth. "Oh, ha ha, I thought you lost your tongue."

We went on to school. I sank down into my seat, my head on my arms. "June T, are you all right?" Mr. Morrisey asked. I nodded. My head was almost too heavy to lift.

The Other June went to the pencil sharpener. Round and round she whirled the handle. Walking back, looking at me, she held the three sharp pencils like three little knives.

Someone knocked on the door. Mr. Morrisey went out into the hall. Paper planes burst into the air, flying from desk to desk. Someone turned on a transistor radio. And the Other June, coming closer, smiled and licked her lips like a cat sleepily preparing to gulp down a mouse.

I remembered my dream of kicking her, punching, biting her like a dog.

Then my mother spoke quickly in my ear: *Turn the other cheek, my Junie, smile at the world and the world'll surely smile back.*

But I had turned the other cheek, and it was slapped. I had smiled, and the world hadn't smiled back. I couldn't run home as fast as my feet would take me; I had to stay in school—and in school there was the Other June. Every morning, there would be the Other June, and every afternoon, and every day, all day, there would be the Other June.

She frisked down the aisle, stabbing the pencils in the air toward me. A boy stood up on his desk and bowed. "My fans," he said, "I greet you." My arm twitched and throbbed, as if the Other June's pencils had already poked through the skin. She came closer, smiling her Tuesday smile.

"No," I whispered, "*no.*" The word took wings and flew me to my feet, in front of the Other June. "*Noooooo.*" It flew out of my mouth into her surprised face.

The boy on the desk turned toward us. "You said something, my devoted fans?"

"No," I said to the Other June. "Oh, no! No. No. No. No more." I pushed away the hand that held the pencils.

The Other June's eyes opened, popped wide like the eyes of somebody in a cartoon. It made me laugh. The boy on the desk laughed, and then the other kids were laughing, too.

"No," I said again, because it felt so good to say it. "No, no, no, no." I leaned toward the Other June, put my finger against her chest. Her cheeks turned red, she squawked something—it sounded like "Eeeraaghyou!"—and she stepped back. She stepped away from me.

The door banged, the airplanes disappeared, and Mr. Morrisey walked to his desk. "Okay. Okay. Let's get back to work. Kevin Clark, how about it?" Kevin jumped off the desk, and Mr. Morrisey picked up a piece of chalk.

"All right, class—" He stopped and looked at me and the Other June. "You two Junes, what's going on there?"

I tried it again. My finger against her chest. Then the words. "No—more." And she stepped back another step. I sat down at my desk.

"June M," Mr. Morrisey said.

She turned around, staring at him with that big-eyed cartoon look. After a moment she sat down at her desk with a loud slapping sound.

Even Mr. Morrisey laughed.

And sitting at my desk, twirling my braids, I knew this was the last Tuesday of the Other June.

"My name is Prot, and this is my brother Krot."

Prot and Krot

Polish folktale
as told by Agnes Szudek

There was once a soldier who had been away from Poland for many years fighting in the war with Sweden. When the war was over, he took a ship for home and it cost him nearly all his money. By the time he arrived at the port of Danzig, he had only two coins in his pocket, a small loaf of bread in his knapsack, and nothing else.

His home was in the south near Sandomiersh, by the river Vistula, and he thought he would follow the river on foot, since he could not afford to sail or ride.

He had not gone far when he came to a churchyard where two old men sat together on a bench. They looked at the soldier as he passed by.

"Hello there, fine soldier boy!" one of them called. "God be with you."

"And with you," answered the soldier, raising his cap.

"Tell us, laddie, where you have been soldiering?" asked the second old man.

The soldier was anxious to be on his way, but he was a civil fellow, so he stopped out of politeness. "I've been in many places, fighting the Swedes," he said. "Now I'm on my way home to Sandomiersh."

"Ah, it must be good to have a home to go to," said the first old man. "Some people have all the luck in the world. My name is Prot, and this is my brother Krot."

"Yes, yes, I'm Krot and he's Prot. At least we think so, but we're never quite sure. Anyway, what does it matter? Our trouble is that we have neither home, food, nor even a penny between us."

"Well, I've only two pennies left," said the soldier, drawing the coins from his purse. "You can have them if they're any use to you." He gave the money to the old men, and their eyes twinkled with merriment as they exchanged looks.

"We won't forget you, soldier boy," they said. "It's good to know there's a little kindness left in the world."

The soldier saluted his elders and went on his way, whistling gaily. It was a long walk to Sandomiersh, and after traveling for many hours he felt tired and hungry. His old boots had trodden many battlefields, and they were now so full of holes that he could hardly walk in them.

"A bite of bread's the order of the day now, I think," he said to himself, taking the rye bread from his knapsack. He was about to cut off a piece with his knife when he heard someone calling him.

"Hello there, soldier boy!"

The soldier turned his head in the direction of the river, from where the voice came, and there he saw Prot and Krot floating past on a simple raft made of bits of wood tied together with rope.

He gave them a wave, then noticed something quite extraordinary about the raft. It was moving upstream, against the current—without help from anyone! The soldier hurried alongside and called out, "Where did you find such a raft?"

"Oh, here and there. Bits and pieces we bought with the money you gave us," Prot called back.

"That's right, bits and pieces," echoed Krot. "We're still hungry. Have you got anything to eat?"

"Only a small loaf," answered the soldier. "You're welcome to share it."

"Then jump aboard. We're going your way as you see," said Prot.

"Going your way," said Krot.

So the soldier jumped on the raft, and the three of them shared the bread, which was very little indeed, and they had nothing to drink. But the old men did not complain. They were surprisingly good companions.

"Tell us, soldier boy, what would you wish for if you could have anything in the world?" asked Prot.

"Ah, that would take a lot of thought," replied the soldier, tapping his pipe to clean it out a bit. "There's not much in the world I really need."

"Surely there must be something," insisted Prot. "Treasure and a fine manor house, perhaps?"

"Oooooooh yes! Treasure and a manor house," said Krot.

"No, no, nothing like that. I wouldn't know how to be a grand gentleman. No, thank you, but I'd like a nice pipeful of tobacco and perhaps a few coins in my purse. That would satisfy me, I think," said the soldier.

"Go on, soldier boy, think harder," urged Prot. "Anything in the world."

"Yes, much harder. Anything at all," said Krot.

The soldier touched the knapsack with his foot. "Well," he said slowly, "since I don't want to own much more than a knapsack, it would be useful if it could hold anything, or even anyone, just for the asking. What do you think of that?"

"Not bad, not bad," said Prot.

"Not bad," said Krot. "Such wishes might come true."

"Oh yes," laughed the soldier. "Like pie in the sky, or wine in the brine, no doubt."

No sooner had he spoken than a big round pie appeared in the sky over their heads. Down it came and settled itself on the raft; shiny brown, crusty, and filled with tender beef and vegetables. At the same time, in the water there appeared three bottles of red wine, knocking themselves against the raft as though begging to be opened.

Prot and Krot and the soldier ate the delicious pie, and washed it down with a bottle of red wine each. The soldier was astonished by the appearance of the food and drink, but he was so hungry, he ate first and thought to ask questions afterward. As they finished their meal, the raft was nearing Sandomiersh.

"Time for you to get off," said Prot.

"Yes, off you go," said Krot.

The soldier picked up his knapsack and leapt onto the green bank. "Goodbye and thank you," he called back. "But do tell me where . . ." He looked up and down the river, but there was no raft to be seen and no Prot and Krot. The expanse of the Vistula was empty, save for a heron diving low over the water, and a kingfisher waiting motionless on a log.

"Such things could only happen in a dream," muttered the soldier, rubbing his eyes. "I must have been walking in my sleep."

He slung his small pack over his shoulder and put his pipe in his mouth, although there was no tobacco in it. As he sucked away absentmindedly, the pipe began to smoke, and the scent of sweet tobacco came from the bowl.

"Heavens above! Prot and Krot!" cried the soldier, looking about him as though he expected the two old men to be lurking in the grass. "Wherever you are, I thank you for your kindness." There was no sound in the quiet countryside, but the smoke from the pipe shaped itself into words which spelled out:

"YOUR KINDNESS IS REWARDED."

The soldier went on his way wondering who the strange old men could be. By evening he came to an inn where he thought he would ask for a drink of water, since he had no money for anything else. As he walked through the doorway, the purse in his belt began to feel heavier and heavier. On opening it he found that it was full of gold pieces! He ate a good supper of boiled beef in horseradish sauce, and cheese pancakes, and as he took a coin from his purse to pay the innkeeper, another one immediately came in its place. His second wish had come true!

Now the soldier did not know it, but sitting near him was a robber who saw the gold and made up his mind to have the purse. He waited in a dark corner outside the inn, ready to spring. When the soldier came out, night had fallen and before he knew what was happening the robber jumped out and demanded the money.

"My money?" said the surprised soldier.

"That's it! The gold in your purse. I saw it and I'll have it, or I'll have your life," snarled the robber.

The soldier thought quickly about his third wish, which might, only *might*, just come true. He decided to try it.

"I have put the purse in my knapsack," he said. "Take it by all means." Swinging his pack to the ground, he unfastened the buckle. As the robber bent down, the soldier said, "Into my knapsack and stay there."

As quick as lightning, the robber shot head first into the knapsack and was stuck fast. The soldier hoisted him onto his back and tipped him into the well in front of the inn.

"*Splash*!" Down he went to the bottom, and the soldier wound down the rope and the bucket. "Sit in the bucket," he shouted. "Someone may pull you up, if you're lucky," and away he went.

The night was warm and the sky was bright with a sprinkling of stars. The soldier took the road home, which ran close to the castle of the king. He remembered how as a boy he used to watch hundreds of candles flickering in the windows and wonder what the royal family was doing.

Shortly before he reached the castle walls he saw a curious sight in a turnip field. There among the ripe turnips stood a round golden tent, guarded by a circle of the king's guards. On the hill above rose the royal castle without a single light shining in any of its windows. The soldier thought this strange and stopped to inquire.

"What's wrong?" he asked. "The castle looks deserted."

"So it is and likely to be for many a year," said one of the guards. "His Majesty can no longer live there."

"But why?" asked the soldier.

"Surely everyone in these parts knows by now that the castle is haunted by a demon that will not give the king peace, day or night. No one can get rid of it, no one at all, and the king can bear it no more."

"I think perhaps I may be able to help the king," said the soldier obligingly.

"I would be indebted to you all my life if you could," said the king, emerging from his tent in his nightgown.

The astonished soldier fell upon his knees. "Your Majesty, let me go to the castle tonight before I return home, and I will rid you of the demon."

"My dear fellow," said the king, straightening his nightcap, "you don't know what you are saying. You, go there alone, when I and all my courtiers could not bear it? No, no, it is too much to ask. I cannot allow it."

"Perhaps Your Majesty is fond of camping out?" ventured the soldier.

"Not in the least, dear boy! It's so unroyal, don't you see? And most uncomfortable," replied the king, patting his aching back.

"Then let me help. I only ask permission to sleep in the castle tonight, that's all."

The king could hardly refuse. He went into his tent, and returned with a huge key. "There you are," he said. "This key will open the door. Go if you must, and if you succeed, you may have any part of my kingdom you wish as a reward."

The soldier thanked the king, took the key, and went up the hill to the darkened castle. He put the key in the lock and let himself into the main hall, where he thought he would spend the night. Taking off his jacket, he put it under his head, and with his knapsack close beside him, he lay down to sleep.

He had scarcely closed his eyes when he was awakened by a shrieking and howling, and a thin high voice calling in the darkness: "Get out! Get out! This is my castle. Everybody out! Clear the way, clear the way. Not even a mouse is allowed to stay. *It is all mine!*"

The soldier opened his eyes, and by the light of the moon, he saw a small figure prancing about. It seemed to be dressed in black, with pointed ears, pointed nose, and long pointed toes. As it went about lifting its knees up to its chin, it saw the figure of the soldier in the corner.

"I said everybody out!" screamed the demon. "Out of here this instant, do you hear? *Out! Out! Out!*"

The soldier was not at all afraid. "Why should I get out?" he said, yawning. "The king has given me permission to sleep here."

"This is my castle now," replied the demon, bouncing up onto the mantelpiece and glaring down at the soldier. "If you don't go I'll—I'll turn you into a fly."

"Then I'll buzz up and down your long nose," said the soldier, lying down again as if he didn't care.

"Will you then, you impudent creature! In that case I'll turn you into a beetle," yelled the demon, stamping up and down on the mantelpiece.

The soldier simply stretched himself and said casually, "What a pleasure it will be for me then to nip all your long pointed toes."

"*What!!!* I'll turn you into a . . . a . . . a . . ."

But before the demon could think of anything else to say, the soldier stood up and said quickly, "I'll turn *you* into my knapsack this very instant and you will remain there until I let you go."

Whizz! With the speed of an arrow the demon shot off the mantelpiece, straight into the knapsack, and the soldier fastened the buckle!

"Let me out of here, whoever you are!" the demon cried.

The soldier took no notice. He put the knapsack under his jacket, put his head down on the jacket, and went to sleep. He was so tired that even the violent kicking of the demon did not disturb him.

In the morning the king sent a troop of his guards to find out what had happened to the brave soldier.

The men peered through the window and saw the soldier sitting on his small pack, peacefully smoking his pipe. Still they did not dare to go in, so they tapped on the window and shouted:

"Are you all right?"

"I'm very well, thank you," replied the soldier.

"Did you see the demon?"

"Yes, of course I did," said the soldier, blowing smoke rings.

"Where is it now?" asked the soldiers, fearfully glancing about them.

"Why, I'm sitting on it," answered the soldier. "Now no more questions if you please. Go and bring me forty blacksmiths with hammers and a barrel of wine."

"*Bring what?*" gasped the soldiers.

"You heard me. Quickly, do as I say." The soldier was beginning to lose patience with the frightened men. Away galloped the guards and they returned two hours later with forty blacksmiths in a cart, and behind them a wagon containing forty hammers and a barrel of wine.

The soldier ordered the blacksmiths to take it in turns hammering on his knapsack, which they did without knowing why. When they were thirsty they took a drink from the barrel, then hammered away with a will.

The demon in the knapsack began to squeal with terror. "Stop it, stop it, d'you hear? You'll never hurt a demon with a hammer, or a hundred hammers, or a thousand hammers, or even a million hammers. Demons can't feel hammers—Ouch!"

"What did you say?" called the soldier above the noise.

"I said you'll never, *ouch*! Hurt me, *ouch*! Never, *oooo-heeyerooh*!!! Stop it, I can't bear it any more!" screeched the demon, who could indeed feel every single blow from the hammers.

"That's what His Majesty said about you," shouted the soldier. "If you promise to leave this land and never return, the hammering will stop. The king wishes to live at peace in his castle."

For a moment the demon said nothing, then a few extra hard blows persuaded him.

"That's enough. I promise. I promise. Have mercy on me. Let me go and I'll never come back."

The hammering stopped and the soldier opened his knapsack. "Come out," he said. A long black pointed toe emerged, then an arm, a long nose, and two green eyes looked out in fear.

"Hurry up before I change my mind," said the soldier sternly.

At once the creature sprang up like a frog and ran away at top speed, down the hill and across the fields until it disappeared in the distance.

The soldier went to the king, who was eating breakfast rolls in his tent.

"You must be the bravest soldier in my entire kingdom," he said when he heard the story.

"Not really, Your Majesty, only the most fortunate," smiled the soldier, thinking of Prot and Krot.

"Say what you like, but I shall raise you to the rank of general. Not a word! It's the very least you deserve," announced the king, offering a plate to the soldier. "Have a roll, and put one in your pocket. Now I shall keep my promise to you. Tell me which part of my kingdom you would like for your own and it shall be yours."

The soldier, who was not a greedy man, took only one roll and asked for very little. "You are most kind, sire," he said bowing. "If it pleases Your Majesty, I need only the little cottage I already own, but if my land could reach down as far as the Vistula river, a matter of three hundred yards or so, then I would be more than content."

"Ah ha! I see you are a fisherman at heart," laughed the king. "You are an easy man to please. I wish there were more like you. From this moment on, the land is yours with the Vistula as its border. And remember, you are most welcome at my castle whenever you wish to come."

The soldier thanked the king, bowed again, and went home at last to his little cottage.

Every day he went to sit on the banks of the Vistula, not, however, to fish, as the king had thought. He puffed his pipe, which was always full of tobacco, and scanned the water for signs of a roughly made raft floating upstream, carrying Prot and Krot. He watched for many months and many years, but he never saw them again. He did not forget them, though, for they had given him all he needed to be happy for the rest of his life, and he lived to the age of one-hundred-and-one!

"Oh, Peerless Ginger Cat! Catch a fish for me!"

Chin Yu Min and the Ginger Cat

Jennifer Armstrong

Many years ago, in a village near Kunming, there lived an official of the government named Secretary Chin. In his house by the lake were the finest lacquer bowls, lettered scrolls of the sheerest paper, and many, many strings of cash. Secretary Chin was very prosperous.

The wife of this man, Chin Yu Min, felt that this prosperity was only what she deserved. She was proud and haughty, and she made her servants perform impossible and meaningless tasks—such as collecting incense smoke in a bamboo cage or teaching carp to strut like roosters—just for the fun of displaying her power. She laughed at beggars and turned them away from her door.

One day Secretary Chin fell out of his small yellow pleasure boat and sank like a piece of carved jade to the bottom of the lake. That was the end of Secretary Chin, and it was also the end of his wife's idleness and luxury.

"Good Chin Yu Min," said her neighbors, "please allow us to help you in this time of loss."

"Aiyi!" Chin Yu Min scoffed. "I don't need help from such as you. Be off!"

She slammed the door in their faces and stomped away. For many months Chin Yu Min scolded her servants and haggled suspiciously with the merchants. She was sure that everyone was out to cheat her, and she answered their pleasant words with bitter ones.

Coin by square-holed coin, her strings of cash flowed away like streams from a fishpond. Chin Yu Min knew she would soon be poor, but she would rather have eaten ashes than let anyone know of this fact.

"Aiyi!" Chin Yu Min screamed at her servants. "You are all less than useless! Leave my house!" When they had gone, she lived alone and tended house with her own hands to save money.

"Esteemed Chin Yu Min," said her neighbors, "allow us to help you."

"Who asked for your help?" Chin Yu Min retorted.

She slammed the door in their faces and stomped away.

Chin Yu Min lived alone for several more months, becoming poorer and poorer. At last she was as poor as a mouse in a monastery.

Not one chicken scratched in her yard. Her rice jar stood cracked and empty. The fine lacquer bowls were dulled by hard use, and the lettered scrolls of sheerest paper flapped like ragged ghosts from the walls.

One morning when Chin Yu Min awoke, she knew there was not a thing in the house to eat. She knew there was no cash with which to buy rice.

"I will fish," Chin Yu Min announced to her empty house and the tattered scrolls.

With this decision firmly made, Chin Yu Min took a string and a hairpin for a hook and went to the lake. She stood straight and aloof, arms out, eyes forward, line dangling, and waited—oh, for only a little while—before scowling with impatience.

"There are no fish in this lake!" she complained.

But below the surface of the water many fish indeed shuttled back and forth like monkeys at play in the treetops. Chin Yu Min shook her fist at the fish and called them uncivil names.

Then a melodious splash caught her ear.

"Aiyi!" Chin Yu Min whispered.

On the next dock sat a fine ginger cat. He draped his long elegant tail into the water, and

flick!

Out it came with a fish biting the end. The cat regarded the fish with a solemn look, blinked, and then quickly ate every bit, scales, fins, and all.

"Oh, Peerless Ginger Cat!" said Chin Yu Min. "Catch a fish for me!"

The ginger cat blinked his eyes. "Certainly, Auntie."

He draped his long elegant tail into the water, and *flick!*

Out it came with a fish on the end.

Chin Yu Min picked it up and sniffed deeply. "Steamed with ginger and soy sauce, this will be delicious."

Chin Yu Min hurried back to her house with the fish and put it on to cook. But as the aromatic steam curled up around her gray-haired head, Chin Yu Min began to worry.

"I have a fish today, but what will I have tomorrow?" she asked herself.

She peeked out the window. The ginger cat was still sitting on the dock, meditating on a pair of mandarin ducks who swam in graceful harmony through the reeds.

Chin Yu Min had an idea.

"Oh, Gracious Ginger Cat!" the greedy woman said, joining him on the dock. "My house is large, my bed is soft. Why not come and live with me? There you will be safe from dogs, cool in the summer, and warm in the winter. All I ask is that you continue to catch fish."

"I thank you, Venerable Auntie," said the cat. "I accept your offer. You are truly generous."

Chin Yu Min smiled a thin smile and hurried back to her house.

From that day Chin Yu Min's prosperity returned. Surely, her neighbors agreed, she had found a charm to make fish jump from the lake into her basket, for every day she arrived at the market with a load of glittering, glistening fish. Her neighbors looked on as Chin Yu Min hung new scrolls with the characters of "Wise Decision" and "Good Management" on her door, and admired the new lacquer bowls that she bought from the merchants. Chin Yu Min was prosperous indeed.

Every day in the afternoon the ginger cat sat on the dock and draped his long elegant tail into the water and

flick!

He pulled out fish after fish until they were piled up like the mountains of Guilin. Chin Yu Min rubbed her hands together and counted her strings of cash.

"Auntie," said the ginger cat one day, "what would you do if I went away?"

"Aiyi!" gasped Chin Yu Min. "Don't leave me! How would I eat?"

Chin Yu Min wrung her hands. She could not bear another plunge into poverty.

"I will stay, Auntie," replied the ginger cat.

In the evenings of the warm months, Chin Yu Min sat in front of her door watching the lake with the ginger cat at her side. From time to time the sound of his purring broke the stillness, and Chin Yu Min was content as she watched the cranes fly overhead.

In the evenings of the cool months, Chin Yu Min sat in front of a fire in the house watching the coals with the ginger cat at her side. From time to time the sound of his purring broke the stillness, and Chin Yu Min was content as she watched the embers glow at her feet.

"Auntie," said the ginger cat one day, "what would you do if I went away?"

"Aiyi!" gasped Chin Yu Min. She hastily stroked his back. "Don't do that to an old woman!"

Chin Yu Min wrung her hands. She could not bear another plunge into solitude.

"I will stay, Auntie," replied the ginger cat.

One day a beggar came to the door.

"Please, Virtuous Lady," he said, "have you an old basket in which I may carry my meager belongings?"

"Pah!" said Chin Yu Min. "Filthy beggar! There, take that ragged thing. It's of no use to me."

So saying, she pointed at a torn and tattered basket that lay discarded in the sun.

"Blessings upon you," the beggar said. He hoisted the basket above his head and limped off to town.

Chin Yu Min cast a thoughtful glance out at the lake. It was time for the ginger cat to start fishing for the day.

"Honorable Ginger Cat!" she called out. "Where are you?"

The answer was wind soughing through the trees.

"Delightful Ginger Cat!" she called again. "Where are you?"

The answer was wavelets lapping the pebbled shore. The ginger cat was nowhere.

"He has left me!" Chin Yu Min cried out.

She stood stricken in the doorway, staring at her fine scrolls. "Wise Decision" and "Good Management" mocked her as they rustled in the breeze.

"No more fish!" Chin Yu Min despaired.

The scrolls rustled again.

"No more prosperity!"

The scrolls shivered.

"No more sitting by the fire!"

The scrolls flapped forlornly.

"No more purring!"

The scrolls fell from their hooks.

"No more fine ginger cat to sit beside me!"

Chin Yu Min tore at her hair. "Wise Decision" and "Good Management" lay in shreds at her feet. In despair Chin Yu Min took up a brush and wrote the characters for "Bottomless Sorrow" on her door.

"Have you seen my ginger cat?" Chin Yu Min asked the neighbors. "Help me find my ginger cat!"

Her neighbors frowned. "When we offered you our help, Chin Yu Min, you scorned us."

"I beseech you," Chin Yu Min said. "Most humbly I ask, have you seen my ginger cat?"

"We have not," her neighbors said, taking pity on her bottomless sorrow. "But we have seen a beggar with an old basket pass this way. Perhaps he knows something."

Chin Yu Min stood as still as a plum tree rooted to the ground. As sure as the sun rose and set, she knew that the ginger cat had been sleeping in the basket. She had given him away.

"Where, oh, where has the beggar gone?" Chin Yu Min asked her neighbors.

"To the market," they replied.

Chin Yu Min ran as fast as her skinny old legs would carry her to the market. There, to her amazement, she found many, many beggars, each with a tattered basket. To her, all beggars looked alike, because she had always been too proud to see their faces.

Now she did not know which one had her basket.

"I beg you," she said to the first, "Venerable Old Monk, allow me to buy your basket."

The beggar bowed once and pulled on his thin gray beard. "For ten cash, madam."

Chin Yu Min gritted her teeth. But her ginger cat was worth more than that in fish. She paid the beggar and snatched the basket: empty.

"I beg you," she said to the next, "Spiritual Old Monk, allow me to buy your basket."

The beggar bowed once and tugged his short stubby beard. "For ten cash, madam."

Chin Yu Min gritted her teeth. But her ginger cat was worth more than that in fish. She paid the beggar and snatched the basket: empty.

"I beg you," she said to the third, "Self-Denying Old Monk, allow me to buy your basket."

Before each beggar she humbled herself and paid for the baskets. Her strings of cash were vanishing like water into sand. The longer she searched for her cat, the more desolate she became.

"For ten cash," said another beggar.

Chin Yu Min pulled at her hair. But all the fish in the Middle Kingdom were not equal to her ginger cat. He was worth far, far more in companionship and warmth.

"Ten cash," said the next.

"Ten cash," said another.

At last she had not one single coin left, and Chin Yu Min was as poor as the beggars—even poorer, for each of them had ten cash, and she had none. But more bitter than the loss of her cash was the loss of her cat.

"Let him not catch another fish!" she cried to heaven. "But still let my friend come back to live with me!"

In tears, Chin Yu Min turned away from the market and trod wearily back to the lake. But before she reached her home, she saw another beggar ahead on the road. This beggar, too, had an old basket.

"Most Scholarly Old Monk," cried the proud Chin Yu Min, "pity an old woman as poor as you! I beg you to give me your basket."

Chin Yu Min knelt in the road and kowtowed with her forehead to the dust. Her heart cried out for the ginger cat.

"Certainly, madam," the beggar said. "If I can take away your bottomless sorrow in this way, I will give you my basket."

So saying, he placed the basket on the ground beside her and hobbled away.

Fear shook Chin Yu Min's hands as she opened the basket. Her breath quaked in her throat.

Inside, curled in sleep, was the ginger cat.

"Oh, Generous Friend!" Chin Yu Min cried. "I have found you again!"

"Good afternoon, Auntie," said the ginger cat, stretching his legs. "Isn't it time to fish?"

For her answer Chin Yu Min hugged the cat to her heart.

"Today I fish for you," she said.

With the cat perched on her shoulder, Chin Yu Min walked back to her home. At the doors of her neighbors, she stopped and bowed.

"Please honor me by taking a meal at my house," she said. "My table is poor, but your presence will make it seem rich to me."

Her neighbors returned her bows and accepted with thanks.

And from that time the scrolls on Chin Yu Min's door read "Contented Joy."

The whole town talked about the marvelous bird.

THE NIGHTINGALE

Hans Christian Andersen

In China, as you know, the Emperor is Chinese, and so are his court and all his people. This story happened a long, long time ago; and that is just the reason why you should hear it now, before it is forgotten. The Emperor's palace was the most beautiful in the whole world. It was made of porcelain and had been most costly to build. It was so fragile that you had to be careful not to touch anything, and that can be difficult. The gardens were filled with the loveliest flowers; the most beautiful of them had little silver bells that tinkled so you wouldn't pass by without noticing them.

Everything in the Emperor's garden was most cunningly arranged. The gardens were so large that even the head gardener did not know exactly how big they were. If you kept walking you finally came to the most beautiful forest, with tall trees that mirrored themselves in deep lakes. The forest stretched all the way to the sea, which was blue and so deep that even large boats could sail so close to the shore that they were shaded by the trees. Here lived a nightingale who sang so sweetly that even the fisherman, who came every night to set his nets, would stop to rest when he heard it, and say, "Blessed God, how beautifully it sings!" But he couldn't listen too long, for he had work to do, and soon he would forget the bird. Yet the next night when he heard it again, he would repeat what he had said the night before: "Blessed God, how beautifully it sings!"

From all over the world travelers came to the Emperor's city to admire his palace and gardens; but when they heard the nightingale sing, they all declared that it was the loveliest of all. When they returned to their own countries, they would write long and learned books about the city, the palace, and the garden; but they didn't forget the nightingale. No, that was always mentioned in the very first chapter. Those who could write poetry wrote long odes about the nightingale who lived in the forest on the shores of the deep blue sea.

These books were read the whole world over, and finally one was also sent to the Emperor. He sat down in his golden chair and started to read it. Every once in a while, he would nod his head because it pleased him to read how his own city and his own palace and gardens were praised; but then he came to the sentence, "But the song of the nightingale is the loveliest of all."

"What!" said the Emperor. "The nightingale? I don't know it, I have never heard of it, and yet it lives not only in my empire but in my very garden. That is the sort of thing one can only find out by reading books."

He called his chief courtier, who was so very noble that if anyone of a rank lower than his own, either talked to him or dared ask him a question, he only answered, "P." And that didn't mean anything at all.

"There is a strange and famous bird called the nightingale," began the Emperor. "It is thought to be the most marvelous thing in my empire. Why have I never heard of it?"

"I have never heard of it," answered the courtier. "It has never been presented at court."

"I want it to come this evening and sing for me," demanded the Emperor. "The whole world knows of it, but I do not."

"I have never heard it mentioned before," said the courtier, and bowed. "But I shall search for it and find it."

But that was more easily said than done. The courtier ran all through the palace, up the stairs and down the stairs and through the long corridors, but none of the people whom he asked had ever heard of the nightingale. He returned to the Emperor and declared that the whole story was nothing but a fable, invented by those people who had written the books. "Your Imperial Majesty should not believe everything that is written. A discovery is one thing and artistic imagination something quite different; it is fiction."

"The book I have just read," replied the Emperor, "was sent to me by the great Emperor of Japan; and therefore, every word in it must be the truth. I want to hear the nightingale! And that tonight! If it does not come, then the whole court shall have their stomachs thumped, and that right after they have eaten."

"Tsing-pe!" said the courtier. He ran again up and down the stairs and through the corridors; and half the court ran with him, because they didn't want their stomachs thumped. Everywhere they asked about the nightingale that the whole world knew about, and yet no one at court had heard of.

At last they came to the kitchen, where a poor little girl worked, scrubbing the pots and pans. "Oh, I know the nightingale," she said. "I know it well; it sings so beautifully. Every evening I am allowed to bring some leftovers to my poor sick mother who lives down by the sea. Now it is far away, and as I return I often rest in the forest and listen to the nightingale. I get tears in my eyes from it, as though my mother were kissing me."

"Little kitchen maid," said the courtier, "I will arrange for a permanent position in the kitchen for you and permission to see the Emperor eat, if you will take us to the nightingale; it is summoned to court tonight."

Half the court went to the forest to find the nightingale. As they were walking along, a cow began to bellow.

"Oh!" shouted all the courtiers. "There it is. What a marvelously powerful voice the little animal has; we have heard it before."

"That is only a cow," said the little kitchen maid. "We are still far from where the nightingale lives."

They passed a little pond; the frogs were croaking.

"Lovely," sighed the Chinese Imperial Dean. "I can hear her; she sounds like little church bells ringing."

"No, that is only the frogs," said the little kitchen maid, "but any time now we may hear it."

Just then the nightingale began singing.

"There it is!" said the little girl. "Listen. Listen. It is up there on that branch." And she pointed to a little gray bird sitting amid the greenery.

"Is that possible?" exclaimed the chief courtier. "I had not imagined it would look like that. It looks so common! I think it has lost its color from shyness and out of embarrassment at seeing so many noble people at one time."

"Little nightingale," called the kitchen maid, "our Emperor wants you to sing for him."

"With pleasure," replied the nightingale, and sang as lovely as he could.

"It sounds like little glass bells," sighed the chief courtier. "Look at its little throat, how it throbs. It is strange that we have never heard of it before; it will be a great success at court."

"Shall I sing another song for the Emperor?" asked the nightingale, who thought that the Emperor was there.

"Most excellent little nightingale," began the chief courtier, "I have the pleasure to invite you to attend the court tonight, where His Imperial Majesty, the Emperor of China, wishes you to enchant him with your most charming art."

"It sounds best in the green woods," said the nightingale; but when he heard that the Emperor insisted, he followed them readily back to the palace.

There, every room had been polished, and thousands of little golden lamps reflected themselves in the shiny porcelain walls and floors. In the corridors stood all the most beautiful flowers, the ones with silver bells on them; and there was such a draft from all the servants running in and out, and opening and closing doors, that all the bells were tinkling and you couldn't hear what anyone said.

In the grand banquet hall, where the Emperor's throne stood, a little golden perch had been hung for the nightingale to sit on. The whole court was there, and the little kitchen maid, who now had the title of Imperial Kitchen Maid, was allowed to stand behind one of the doors and listen. Everyone was dressed in their finest clothes, and they all were looking at the little gray bird, toward which the Emperor nodded very kindly.

The nightingale's song was so sweet that tears came into the Emperor's eyes; and when they ran down his cheeks, the little nightingale sang even more beautifully than it had before. His song spoke to one's heart, and the Emperor was so pleased that he ordered his golden slipper to be hung around the little bird's neck. There was no higher honor. But the nightingale thanked him and said that he had been honored enough already.

"I have seen tears in the eyes of an emperor, and that is a great enough treasure for me. There is a strange power in an emperor's tears, and God knows that is reward enough." Then he sang yet another song.

"That was the most charming and elegant song we have ever heard," said all the ladies of the court. And from that time onward they filled their mouths with water, so they could make a clucking noise whenever anyone spoke to them, because they thought that then they sounded like the nightingale. Even the chambermaids and the lackeys were satisfied; and that really meant something, for servants are the most difficult to please. Yes, the nightingale was a success.

He was to have his own cage at court and permission to take a walk twice a day and once during the night. Twelve servants were to accompany him; each held on tightly to a silk ribbon that was attached to the poor bird's legs. There wasn't any pleasure in such an outing.

The whole town talked about the marvelous bird. Whenever two people met in the street they would sigh; one would say, "night," and the other, "gale"; and then they would understand each other perfectly. Twelve delicatessen shop owners named their children "Nightingale," but not one of them could sing.

One day a package arrived for the Emperor; on it was written "Nightingale."

"It is probably another book about our famous bird," said the Emperor. But he was wrong; it was a mechanical nightingale. It lay in a little box and was supposed to look like the real one, though it was made of silver and gold and studded with sapphires, diamonds, and rubies. When you wound it up, it could sing one of the songs the real nightingale sang; and while it performed, its little silver tail would go up and down. Around its neck hung a ribbon on which was written, "The Emperor of Japan's nightingale is inferior to the Emperor of China's."

"It is beautiful!" exclaimed the whole court. And the messenger who had brought it had the title of Supreme Imperial Nightingale Deliverer bestowed upon him at once.

"They ought to sing together; it will be a duet," said everyone, and they did. But that didn't work out well at all; for the real bird sang in his own manner, and the mechanical one had a cylinder inside its chest instead of a heart. "It is not its fault," said the Imperial Music Master. "It keeps perfect time; it belongs to my school of music." Then the mechanical nightingale had to sing solo. Everyone agreed that its song was just as beautiful as the real nightingale's; and besides, the artificial bird was much pleasanter to look at, with its sapphires, rubies, and diamonds that glittered like bracelets and brooches.

The mechanical nightingale sang its song thirty-three times and did not grow tired. The court would have liked to hear it the thirty-fourth time, but the Emperor thought that the real nightingale ought to sing now. But where was it? Nobody had noticed that he had flown out through an open window, to his beloved green forest.

"What is the meaning of this!" said the Emperor angrily, and the whole court blamed the nightingale and called him an ungrateful creature.

"But the best bird remains," they said, and the mechanical bird sang its song once more. It was the same song, for it knew no other; but it was very intricate, so the courtiers didn't know it by heart yet. The Imperial Music Master praised the bird and declared that it was better than the real nightingale, not only on the outside where the diamonds were, but also inside.

"Your Imperial Majesty and gentlemen, you understand that the real nightingale cannot be depended upon. One never knows what he will sing; whereas, in the mechanical bird, everything is determined. There is one song and no other! One can explain everything. We can open it up to examine and appreciate how human thought has fashioned the wheels and the cylinder, and put them where they are, to turn just as they should."

"Precisely what I was thinking!" said the whole court in a chorus. And the Imperial Music Master was given permission to show the new nightingale to the people on the following Sunday.

The Emperor thought that they, too, should hear the bird. They did and they were as delighted as if they had gotten drunk on too much tea. It was all very Chinese. They pointed with their licking fingers toward heaven, nodded, and said, "Oh!"

But the poor fisherman, who had heard the real nightingale, mumbled, "It sounds beautiful and like the bird's song, but something is missing, though I don't know what it is."

The real nightingale was banished from the empire.

The mechanical bird was given a silk pillow to rest upon, close to the Emperor's bed, and all the presents it had received were piled around it. Among them were both gold and precious stones. Its title was Supreme Imperial Night-table Singer, and its rank was Number One to the Left—the Emperor thought the left side was more distinguished because that is the side where the heart is, even in an emperor.

The Imperial Music Master wrote a work in twenty-five volumes about the mechanical nightingale. It was not only long and learned but filled with the most difficult Chinese words, so everyone bought it and said they had read and understood it, for otherwise they would have been considered stupid and had to have their stomachs poked.

A whole year went by. The Emperor, the court, and all the Chinese in China knew every note of the Supreme Imperial Night-table Singer's song by heart; but that was the very reason why they liked it so much: they could sing it themselves, and they did. The street urchins sang, "Zi-zi-zizzi, cluck-cluck-cluck-cluck." And so did the Emperor. Oh, it was delightful!

But one evening, when the bird was singing its very best and the Emperor was lying in bed listening to it, something said, "Clang," inside it. It was broken! All the wheels whirred around, and then the bird was still.

The Emperor jumped out of bed and called his physician, but he couldn't do anything, so the Imperial Watchmaker was fetched. With great difficulty he repaired the bird, but he declared that the cylinders were worn and new ones could not be fitted. The bird would have to be spared; it could not be played so often.

It was a catastrophe. Only once a year was the mechanical bird allowed to sing, and then it had difficulty finishing its song. But the Imperial Music Master made a speech wherein he explained, using the most difficult words, that the bird was as good as ever; and then it was.

Five years passed and a great misfortune happened. Although everyone loved the old Emperor, he had fallen ill, and they all agreed that he would not get well again. It was said that a new emperor had already been chosen; and when people in the street asked the chief courtier how the Emperor was, he would shake his head and say, "P."

Pale and cold, the Emperor lay in his golden bed. The whole court believed him to be already dead, and they were busy visiting and paying their respects to the new Emperor. The lackeys were all out in the street gossiping, and the chambermaids were drinking coffee. All the floors in the whole palace were covered with black carpets so that no one's steps would disturb the dying Emperor; and that's why it was as quiet as quiet could be in the whole palace.

But the Emperor was not dead yet. Pale and motionless he lay in his great golden bed; the long velvet drapes were drawn, and the golden tassels moved slowly in the wind, for one of the windows was open. The moon shone down upon the Emperor, and its light reflected in the diamonds of the mechanical bird.

The Emperor could hardly breathe; he felt as though someone were sitting on his chest. He opened his eyes. Death was sitting there. He was wearing the Emperor's golden crown and held his golden saber in one hand and his imperial banner in the other. From the folds of the curtains that hung around his bed, strange faces looked down at the Emperor. Some of them were frighteningly ugly, and others mild and kind. They were the evil and good deeds that the Emperor had done. Now, while Death was sitting on his heart, they were looking down at him.

"Do you remember?" whispered first one and then another. And they told him things that made the cold sweat of fear appear on his forehead.

"No, no, I don't remember! It is not true!" shouted the Emperor. "Music, music, play the great Chinese gong," he begged, "so that I will not be able to hear what they are saying."

But the faces kept talking, and Death, like a real Chinese, nodded his head to every word that was said.

"Little golden nightingale, sing!" demanded the Emperor. "I have given you gold and precious jewels, and with my own hands have I hung my golden slipper around your neck. Sing! Please sing!"

But the mechanical nightingale stood as still as ever, for there was no one to wind it up; and then, it couldn't sing.

Death kept staring at the Emperor out of the empty sockets in his skull; and the palace was still, so terrifyingly still.

All at once the most beautiful song broke the silence. It was the nightingale, who had heard of the Emperor's illness and torment. He sat on a branch outside the Emperor's window and sang to bring him comfort and hope. As he sang, the faces in the folds of the curtains faded, and the blood pulsed with greater force through the Emperor's weak body. Death himself listened and said, "Please, little nightingale, sing on!"

"Will you give me the golden saber? Will you give me the imperial banner? Will you give me the golden crown?"

Death gave each of his trophies for a song; and then the nightingale sang about the quiet churchyard, where white roses grow, where fragrant elderberry trees are, and where the grass is green from the tears of those who come to mourn. Death longed so much for his garden that he flew out of the window, like a white cold mist.

"Thank you, thank you," whispered the Emperor, "you heavenly little bird; I remember you. You have I banished from my empire, and yet you came to sing for me; and when you sang the evil phantoms that taunted me disappeared, and Death himself left my heart. How shall I reward you?"

"You have rewarded me already," said the nightingale. "I shall never forget that, the first time I sang for you, you gave me the tears from your eyes; and to a poet's heart, those are jewels. But sleep so you can become well and strong; I shall sing for you."

The little gray bird sang, and the Emperor slept, so blessedly, so peacefully.

The sun was shining in through the window when he woke; he did not feel ill anymore. None of his servants had come, for they thought that he was already dead; but the nightingale was still there, and he was singing.

"You must come always," declared the Emperor. "I shall only ask you to sing when you want to. And the mechanical bird I shall break in a thousand pieces."

"Don't do that," replied the nightingale. "The mechanical bird sang as well as it could; keep it. I can't build my nest in the palace; let me come to visit you when I want to, and I shall sit on the branch outside your window and sing for you. And my song shall make you happy and make you thoughtful. I shall sing not only of those who are happy but also of those who suffer. I shall sing of the good and of the evil that happen around you, and yet are hidden from you. For a little songbird flies far. I visit the poor fishermen's cottages and the peasant's hut, far away from your palace and your court. I love your heart more than your crown, and yet I feel that the crown has a fragrance of something holy about it. I will come! I will sing for you! Only one thing must you promise me."

"I will promise you anything," said the Emperor, who had dressed himself in his imperial clothes and was holding his golden saber and pressing it against his heart.

"I beg of you never tell anyone that you have a little bird that tells you everything, for then you will fare even better." And with those words the nightingale flew away.

The servants entered the room to look at their dead master. There they stood gaping when the Emperor said, "Good morning."

"Not now," Dan said quietly. "Later."

FRESH

Philippa Pearce

The force of water through the river gates scoured to a deep bottom; then the river shallowed again. People said the pool below the gates was very deep. Deep enough to drown in anyway.

At the bottom of the pool lived the freshwater mussels. No one had seen them there—most people would not have been particularly interested in them anyway. But if you were poking about among the stones in the shallows below the pool, you couldn't help finding mussel shells occasionally. Sometimes one by itself; sometimes two still hinged together. Grey-blue or green-grey on the outside; on the inside, a faint sheen of mother-of-pearl.

The Webster boys were fishing with their nets in the shallows for minnows, freshwater shrimps—anything that moved—when they found a freshwater mussel that was not just a pair of empty shells.

Dan Webster found it. He said, "Do you want this shell? It's double." While Laurie Webster was saying, "Let's see," Dan was lifting it and had noticed that the two shells were clamped together and that they had unusual weight. "They're not empty shells," he said. "They've something inside. It's alive."

He stooped again to hold the mussel in the palm of his hand so that the river water washed over it. Water creatures prefer water.

Laurie had splashed over to him. Now he crouched with the river lapping near the tops of his Wellington boots. "A freshwater mussel!" he said. "I've never owned one." He put out fingers to touch it—perhaps to take it—as it lay on the watery palm of Dan's hand. Dan's fingers curled up into a protective wall. "Careful," he said.

Together, as they were now, the Webster boys looked like brothers, but they were cousins. Laurie was the visitor. He lived in London and had an aquarium on his bedroom windowsill, instead of a river almost at his back door as Dan had. Dan was older than Laurie; Laurie admired Dan, and Dan was kind to Laurie. They did things together. Dan helped Laurie to find livestock for his aquarium—shrimps, leeches, flatworms, water snails variously whorled; whatever the turned stone and stooping net might bring them. During a visit by Laurie, they would fish often, but—until the last day—without a jam jar, just for the fun of it. On the last day, they took a jam jar and put their more interesting catches into it for Laurie's journey back to London.

Now they had found a freshwater mussel on the second day of Laurie's visit. Five more days still to go.

"We can't keep it," said Dan. "Even if we got the jam jar, it couldn't live in a jam jar for five days. It would be dead by the time you got it back to the aquarium."

Laurie, who was quite young, looked as if he might cry. "I've never had the chance of a freshwater mussel before."

"Well . . ." said Dan. He made as if to put it down among the stones and mud where he had found it.

"Don't! Don't! It's my freshwater mussel! Don't let it go!"

"And don't shout in my ear!" Dan said crossly. "Who said I was letting it go? I was just trying it out in the river again, to see whether it was safe to leave it there. I don't think the current would carry it away."

He put the mussel down in the shelter of a large, slimy stone. The current, breaking on the stone, flowed past without stirring it. But the mussel began to feel at home again. They could almost see it settling contentedly into the mud. After a while it parted the lips of its shells slightly, and a pastrylike substance crowded out a little way.

"What's it *doing*?" whispered Laurie. But this was not the sort of thing that Dan knew, and Laurie would not find out until he got back to his aquarium books in London.

Now they saw that they had not merely imagined the mussel to be settling in. There was less of it visible out of the mud—much less of it.

"It's burying itself. It's escaping," said Laurie. "Don't let it!"

Dan sighed and took the mussel back into the palm of his hand again. The mussel, disappointed, shut up tight.

"We need to keep it in the river," said Dan, "but somewhere where it can't escape."

They looked around. They weren't sure what they were looking for, and at first they certainly weren't finding it.

Still with the mussel in his hand, Dan turned to the banks. They were overhanging, with river water swirling against them and under them. The roots of trees and bushes made a kind of very irregular lattice fencing through which the water ran continually.

"I wonder . . ." said Dan.

"You couldn't keep it there," Laurie said. "It'd be child's play for a freshwater mussel to escape through the roots."

Dan stared at the roots. "I've a better idea," he said. "I'll stay here with the mussel. You go back to our house—to the larder. You'll find a little white plastic carton with Eileen's slimming cress growing in it." Eileen was Dan's elder sister, whose absorbing interest was her figure. "Empty the cress out onto a plate—I'll square Eileen later. Bring the plastic carton back here."

Laurie never questioned Dan. He set off across the meadows towards the house.

Dan and the freshwater mussel were left alone to wait.

Dan was holding the freshwater mussel as he had done before, stooping down to the river with his hand in the water. It occurred to him to repeat the experiment that Laurie had interrupted. He put the mussel down in the lee of the slimy stone again and watched. Again the current left the mussel undisturbed. Again the mussel began to settle itself into the mud between the stones.

Down—gently down—down . . . The freshwater mussel was now as deep in the mud as when Laurie had called out in fear of losing it; but now Laurie was not there. Dan did not interfere. He simply watched the mussel ease itself down—down . . .

Soon less than a quarter of an inch of mussel shell was showing above the mud. The shell was nearly the same colour as the mud embedding it: Dan could identify it only by keeping his eyes fixed continuously upon its projection. That lessened, until it had almost disappeared.

Entirely disappeared . . .

Still Dan stared. As long as he kept his eyes on the spot where the mussel had disappeared, he could get it again. He had only to dig his fingers into the mud at that exact spot to find it. If he let his eyes stray, the mussel was lost forever; there were so many slimy stones like that one, and mud was everywhere. He must keep his eyes fixed on the spot.

"Dan—Dan—Dan!" Laurie's voice came over the meadows. "I've got it!"

He nearly shifted his stare from the spot by the nondescript stone. It would have been so natural to lift his head in response to the calling voice. He was tempted to do it. But he had to remember that this was Laurie's mussel, and it must not be lost; he did remember. He kept his gaze fixed and dug quickly with his fingers and got the mussel again.

There he was standing with the mussel in the palm of his hand, and water and mud dripping from it, when Laurie came in sight. "Is it all right?" he shouted.

"Yes," said Dan.

Laurie climbed down the riverbank into the water with the plastic carton in his hand. Dan looked at it and nodded. "It has holes in the bottom, and we can make some more along the sides with a penknife." He did so, while Laurie held the mussel.

"Now," Dan said, "put the mussel in the carton with some mud and little stones to make it comfortable. That's it. The next thing is to wedge the carton between the roots under the bank at just the right level, so that the water flows through the holes in the carton, without flowing over the whole thing. The mussel will have his flowing river, but he won't be able to escape."

Laurie said, "I wish I could think of things like that."

Dan tried fitting the plastic carton between the roots in several different places, until he found a grip that was just at the right height. Gently he tested the firmness of the wedging, and it held.

"Oh," said Laurie, "it's just perfect, Dan. Thank you. I shall really get it back to the aquarium now. My first freshwater mussel. I shall call it—well, what would *you* call it, Dan?"

"Go on," said Dan. "It's your freshwater mussel. You name it."

"I shall call it Fresh then." Laurie leaned forward to see Fresh, already part buried in his mud, dim in the shadow of the bank, but absolutely a captive. He stood up again and moved back to admire the arrangement from a distance. Then he realized a weakness. "Oh, it'll never do. The plastic's so white. Anyone might notice it and come over to look, and tip Fresh out."

"We'll hide him then," said Dan. He found an old brick among the stones of the shallows and brought it over to the bank roots. He upended the brick in the water, leaning it in a casual pose against the roots, so that it concealed the white plastic carton altogether.

"There," he said.

Laurie sighed. "Really perfect."

"He should be safe there."

"For five days?"

"I tell you what," said Dan, "we could slip down here every day just to have a check on him. To make sure the level of the water through the carton isn't too high or hasn't sunk too low."

Laurie nodded. "Every day."

The daily visit to Fresh was a pleasure that Laurie looked forward to. On the third day it poured with rain, but they put on anoraks as well as boots and made their check as usual. On the fourth day, they reached the riverbank to find a man fishing on the other side of the pool.

The fisherman was minding his own business and only gave them a sidelong glance as they came to a stop on the bank above Fresh's watery dungeon. (They knew its location exactly by now, even from across the meadow.) The man wasn't interested in them—yet. But if they clambered down into the river and began moving old bricks and poking about behind them, he would take notice. He would ask them what they were up to. When they had gone, he would perhaps come over and have a look for himself. He was wearing waders.

"Not now," Dan said quietly. "Later." And they turned away, as though they had come only to look at the view.

They went back after their tea, but the fisherman was still there. In the meantime, Laurie had worked himself into a desperation. "All that rain yesterday has made the river rise. It'll be washing Fresh out of the carton."

"No," said Dan. "You've just got Fresh on the brain. The river's hardly risen at all. If at all. Fresh is all right."

"Why can't that man go home?"

"He'll go home at dusk anyway," said Dan.

"That'll be too late for us. I shall be going to bed by then. You know your mum said I must."

"Yes." Dan looked at him thoughtfully. "Would you like *me* to come? I mean, Mum couldn't stop my being out that bit later than you, because I am that bit older."

"Oh, would you—*would* you?" cried Laurie. "Oh, thanks, Dan."

"Oh, don't thank me," said Dan.

Everything went according to plan, except that Dan, getting down to the river just before dark, found the fisherman still there. But he was in the act of packing up. He did not see Dan. He packed up and walked away, whistling sadly to himself. When the whistling had died away, Dan got down into the river and moved the brick and took out the plastic container. It had been at a safe water level, in spite of the rains, and Fresh was inside, alive and well.

Dan took Fresh out of the carton just to make sure. Then he put him among the stones in the river for the fun of seeing his disappearing act. As he watched, Dan reflected that this was what Fresh would have done if the fisherman *had* spotted the carton and taken him out of it for a good look, and then by mistake dropped him into the water. The fisherman would have lost sight of him, and Fresh would have buried himself. He would have been gone for good—for good, back into the river.

The only signs would have been the brick moved, the plastic container out of place. And Fresh gone. That was all that Dan could have reported to Laurie.

But it had not happened, after all.

Dan picked up Fresh and put him back in the carton and put the carton back, and then the brick, and then walked home. He told Laurie, sitting in his pyjamas in front of the TV with his supper, that everything had been all right. He did not say more.

On the fifth day, the day before Laurie's return to London, they went together to the riverbank. There was no fisherman. The brick was exactly in place and behind it the plastic carton, with the water flowing through correctly. There was Fresh, safe, sound, and apparently not even pining at captivity.

"Tomorrow," said Laurie. "Tomorrow morning we'll bring the jam jar, ready for me to take him home on the train."

That night was the last of Laurie's visit. He and Dan shared Dan's bedroom, and tonight they went to bed at the same time and fell asleep together.

Dan's father was the last person to go to bed at the end of the evening. He bolted the doors and turned out the last lights. That usually did not wake Dan, but tonight it did. Suddenly he was wide awake in the complete darkness, hearing the sound of his parents going to bed in their room, hearing the sound of Laurie's breathing in the next bed, the slow, whispering breath of deep sleep.

The movements and murmurs from the other bedroom ceased; Laurie's breathing continued evenly. Dan still lay wide awake.

He had never really noticed before how very dark everything could be. It was more than blackness; it seemed to fill space as water fills a pool. It seemed to fill the inside of his head.

He lay for some time with the darkness everywhere; then he got up very quietly. He put trousers and sweater on over his pyjamas, bunchily. Laurie's breathing never changed. He tiptoed out of the bedroom and downstairs. In the hall, he put on his Wellington boots. He let himself out of the house and then through the front gate. There was no one about, no lights in the houses, except for a night light where a child slept. There was one lamp in the lane, and that sent his shadow leaping horribly ahead of him. Then he turned a corner and the lamplight had gone. He was taking the short cut towards the river.

No moon tonight. No stars. Darkness . . .

He had been born here; he had always lived here; he knew these meadows as well as he knew himself; but the darkness made him afraid. He could not see the familiar way ahead; he had to remember it. He felt his way. He scented it. He smelled the river before he came to it, and he felt the vegetation changing underfoot, growing ranker when he reached the bank.

He lowered himself into the water, from darkness into darkness. He began to feel along the roots of the bank for the upended brick. He found it quickly—he had not been far out in the point at which he had struck the bank.

His hand was on the brick, and he kept it there while he tried to see. In the darkness and through the darkness, he tried to see what was going to happen—what he was going to make happen. What he was going to do.

Now that he was no longer moving, he could hear the sound of other movements in the darkness.

He heard the water flowing. He heard a *drip* of water into water somewhere near him; a long pause; another *drip*. He heard a quick, quiet birdcall that was strange to him; certainly not an owl—he used to hear those as he lay snug in bed in his bedroom at home. And whatever sound he heard now, he heard beneath it the ceaseless, watery, whispering sound of the river, as if the river were alive and breathing in its sleep in the darkness, like Laurie left sleeping in the bedroom at home.

It was within his power to move the brick and take hold of the plastic carton and tip it right over. Fresh would fall into the water with a *plop* so tiny that he might never hear it above the flow of the river. In such darkness, there would be no question of finding Fresh again, ever.

If he meant to do it, he could do it in three seconds. His hand was on the brick.

But did he mean to do it?

He tried to see what was in his mind, but his mind was like a deep pool of darkness. He didn't know what he really meant to do.

Suddenly he took his hand from the brick and stood erect. He put his booted foot on one of the lateral roots that extended behind the brick. He had to feel for it with his toe. Having found it, he pressed it slowly downwards; then quickly took his foot off again. He could feel the root, released from the pressure, following his foot upwards again in a little jerk.

That jerk of the root might have been enough to upset or at least tilt the carton. It might have been enough to tip Fresh out into the river.

On the other hand, of course, it might not have been enough.

Dan flung himself at the bank well to one side of the brick and clambered up and began a blundering run across the meadows. He did not slow up or go more carefully until he reached the lamplight of the lane and the possibility of someone's hearing his footsteps.

He let himself into the house and secured the door behind him. He left his boots in the hall and his clothes on the chair in the bedroom. He crept back into bed. Laurie was still breathing gently and regularly.

Dan slept late the next morning. He woke to bright sunshine flooding the room and Laurie banging on the bedrail. "Fresh! Fresh! Fresh!" he was chanting. Dan looked at him through eyes half-shut. He was trying to remember a dream he had had last night. It had been a dream of darkness—too dark to remember, or to want to remember. But when he went downstairs to breakfast and saw his boots in the hall with mud still drying on them, he knew that he had not dreamed last night.

Immediately after breakfast, they went down to the river. Laurie was carrying his jam jar.

They climbed down into the shallows as usual. Laurie made a little sound of dismay when he saw the brick. "It's lopsided—the current's moved it!"

Dan stood at a distance in the shallows while Laurie scrabbled the brick down into the water with a splash. There behind it was the white plastic carton, but at a considerable tilt, so that water flowed steadily from its lowest corner. "Oh, Fresh—Fresh!" Laurie implored in a whisper. He was peering into the carton.

"Well?" said Dan, from his distance, not moving.

"Oh, no!" Laurie exclaimed, low but in dismay.

"Well?"

Laurie was poking with a finger at the bottom of the carton. Suddenly he laughed. "He's here after all! It's all right! It was just that burying trick of his! Fresh is here!"

Laurie was beaming.

Dan said, "I'm glad."

Laurie transferred Fresh from the carton to the jam jar, together with some mud and stones and a suitable amount of river water. Dan watched him.

Then they both set off across the meadows again, Laurie holding the jam jar carefully, as he would need to do—as he *would* do—during all the long journey to London. He was humming to himself. He stopped to say to Dan, "I say, I did thank you for Fresh, didn't I?"

"Don't thank me," said Dan.

Dorobo stirred and shivered in his sleep.

THUNDER, ELEPHANT, AND DOROBO

African folktale
as told by Humphrey Harman

The people of Africa say that if you go to the end of a tree (they mean the top) you find more branches than a man can count, but if you go to the beginning (they mean the bottom) you just find two or three, and that is much easier. Nowadays, they say, we are at the end, and there are so many people and so many things that a man doesn't know where to turn for the clutter the world is in, but that in the beginning things were simpler, and fewer, and a man could see between them. For in the beginning there was only the Earth, and on the Earth were just three important things.

The Earth was much as it is now except that there was nothing on it which had been *made*. Only the things that *grow*. If you go into a corner of a forest very early on a warm misty morning then you might get some idea of what the world was like then. Everything very still and vague round the edges, just growing, quietly.

And in this kind of world were three important things.

First there was Elephant. He was very shiny and black because it was a rather wet world, and he lived in the forest where it is always wet. The mist collected on his cold white tusks and dripped slowly off the tips. Sometimes he trampled slowly through the forest, finding leaves and bark and elephant grass and wild figs and wild olives to eat, and sometimes he stood, very tall, very secret, just thinking and listening to the deep, dignified noises in his stomach. When he flapped his great ears it was a gesture, no more. There were no flies.

Then there was Thunder. He was much bigger than Elephant. He was black also, but not a shiny black like Elephant. Sometimes there were streaks of white about him, the kind of white that you get on the belly of a fish. And he had no *shape.* Or, rather, one moment he had one shape, and the next another shape. He was always collecting himself in and spreading himself out like a huge jellyfish. And he didn't walk, he rolled along. He was noisy. Sometimes his voice was very far away, and then it was not so much a sound as a shaking, which Elephant could feel coming up from the ground. It made the drops of mist fall off the leaves and patter on his broad back. But sometimes, when Thunder was in his tight shape, his voice cracked high and angrily, and then Elephant would start and snort and wheel away deeper into the forest. Not because he was frightened, but because it hurt his ears.

And last there was Dorobo.

Dorobo is a man, and if you want to see Dorobo you have to go to Africa, because he lives there still. Even then you won't see him very often because he keeps on the edges of places, and most people like to stay in the middle. He lives where the gardens fade out and the forests begin; he lives where the plains stop and the mountains begin, where the grass dries up and the deserts take over. If you want to see him you had better come quickly, because as more and more things are made there is less and less room for Dorobo. He likes to keep himself to himself, and he's almost over the edge.

He is a small man but very stocky. He is the kind of brown that is almost yellow, and he borrows other people's languages to save himself the bother of making up one of his own. He is always looking steadily for small things that are good at hiding, and because of this the skin round his eyes is crinkled. He makes fire by twirling a pointed stick between the palms of his hands, and then he bends his face sideways and just breathes on a pinch of dried leaf powder and it burns. Fire is about the only thing he does make.

He is very simple and wise, and he was wise then too, when the world was beginning, and he shared it with Elephant and Thunder.

Now these three things were young and new in those days, not quite certain of themselves and rather suspicious of the others because they very seldom met. There was so much room.

One day Thunder came to see Elephant, and after he had rumbled and swelled he settled into the shape that soothed him most, and said, "It's about Dorobo."

Elephant shifted his weight delicately from one foot to the other and said nothing. His ears flapped encouragingly.

"This Dorobo," Thunder went on, "is a strange creature. In fact, so strange that . . . I am leaving the Earth, because I am afraid of him."

Elephant stopped rocking and gurgled with surprise.

"Why?" he asked. "He seems harmless enough to me."

"Listen, Elephant," said Thunder. "When you are sleeping and you get uncomfortable and need to turn upon your other side, what do you do?"

Elephant pondered this. "I stand up," he said at last. "I stand up, and then I lie down again on my other side."

"Well, Dorobo doesn't," said Thunder. "I know. I've watched him. He rolls over without waking up. It's ugly and very strange, and it makes me uncomfortable. The sky, I think, will be a safer home for me."

And Thunder went there. He went straight up, and he's been there ever since. Elephant heard his grumbling die away, and he sucked in his cheeks with astonishment. Then he went to find Dorobo.

It took him three days, but he found him at last, asleep beneath a thorn tree with the grass curled beneath him, like the form of a hare. Elephant rolled slowly forward until he stood right over the sleeping man, and Dorobo lay in his gigantic shadow. Elephant watched him and pondered over all that Thunder had said.

Presently Dorobo stirred and shivered in his sleep. Then he sighed and then he rolled over and curled himself tighter. It was precisely as Thunder had described.

Elephant had never noticed it before. It was strange indeed, but not, he thought, dangerous.

Dorobo opened his eyes and stared up at Elephant and smiled.

"You are clever, Elephant," he said. "I didn't hear you come. You move so silently."

Elephant said nothing.

Dorobo sat up and put his arms round his knees.

"I'm glad you came," he went on. "I've been wanting to speak to you. Do you know Thunder has left us?"

"I had heard that he had gone," replied Elephant.

"Yes," said Dorobo, "I heard him yesterday in the sky. I'm glad and grateful that he's gone, for, to tell you the truth, I was afraid of Thunder. So big, so loud; and you never knew where he might bob up next. Or in what shape. I like things definite."

"He *was* noisy," said Elephant.

"Now you, Elephant, you're quite different. So quiet and kind. Just think, Elephant, now in the whole world there is just you and me, and we shall get on well together because we understand each other."

Then Elephant laughed. He didn't mean to. It rumbled up inside him and took him by surprise. He threw up his trunk and trumpeted. "This ridiculous little creature!"

Then he was ashamed of his bad manners, and he wheeled ponderously and smashed off into the forest, shaking his great head, shaken by enormous bellows of laughter.

"Yes," he shouted back over his shoulder, "we understand . . . ha, ha! . . . understand one another . . . very . . . well!"

He was a good-natured animal, and he didn't want Dorobo to see that he was laughing at him.

But Dorobo had seen, and although the smile stayed on his face, his eyes were very cold and hard and black, like wet pebbles.

Presently he too slipped into the forest, but he walked slowly and looked carefully about him, and after a while he saw the tree he wanted. It was an old white olive tree, a twisted, slow-growing thing, with a very hard, tough wood. Dorobo searched that tree, and after a long time he found a branch that was straight enough and he bent and twisted it until it broke off.

Then he skinned it with his teeth and trimmed it and laid it in the shade to dry. Then he found thin, strong vines hanging from tall trees like rope from a mast, and he tore them down and trailed them behind him to the river. There he soaked them and beat them into cords against the river rocks, and plaited them very tightly together. When his cord was long enough he took his wild olive branch, which was dry now, and strung the first bow. And he bent the bow almost double and let it go, and it sang for him. Next he found straight, stiff sticks, and he made a fire and burned the end of his sticks a little, and rubbed the charred wood off in the sand. This gave them very hard, sharp points.

Taking his bow and his arrows, he ran to the edge of the desert and found the candelabra tree. The candelabra is a strange tree. It has thick, dull green branches that bear no leaves. And the branches stick up in bunches, a little bent, like the fingers of an old man's hand. And when a branch breaks, and it does very easily, it bleeds a white, sticky sap that drips slowly on the sand. You must never shelter beneath a candelabra tree because if the sap drips in your eyes you go blind.

Dorobo broke a branch and dipped his arrows into the thick, milky sap, and twisted them like a spoon in syrup. Then he laid each carefully against a stone to dry.

When everything was ready he went in search of Elephant.

Elephant was asleep under a fig tree, but he woke up when he heard Dorobo's footsteps in the undergrowth. There was something in the way Dorobo walked—something secret and unfriendly that Elephant did not like. For the first time in his life he felt afraid. As quickly as he could he got to his feet and made off through the forest. Dorobo grasped his bow and arrows more firmly and began to follow. Elephant trumpeted to the sky for help. But Thunder growled back, "It is useless to ask for help now. I warned you and you did nothing. You can't tell what a man is thinking by what he *says*, you can only tell by what he *does*. It is too late." From that time to this Dorobo has always hunted Elephant, and so have all men that have come after him.

As for Elephant, he has never again laughed at Dorobo, and has kept as far away from him as he can.

She knew they were dreaming.

All Summer in a Day

Ray Bradbury

"Ready?"

"Ready."

"Now?"

"Soon."

"Do the scientists really know? Will it happen today, will it?"

"Look, look; see for yourself!"

The children pressed to each other like so many roses, so many weeds, intermixed, peering out for a look at the hidden sun.

It rained.

It had been raining for seven years; thousands upon thousands of days compounded and filled from one end to the other with rain, with the drum and gush of water, with the sweet crystal fall of showers and the concussion of storms so heavy they were tidal waves come over the islands. A thousand forests had been crushed under the rain and grown up a thousand times to be crushed again. And this was the way life was forever on the planet Venus, and this was the schoolroom of the children of the rocket men and women who had come to a raining world to set up civilization and live out their lives.

"It's stopping; it's stopping!"

"Yes, yes!"

Margot stood apart from them, from these children who could never remember a time when there wasn't rain and rain and rain. They were all nine years old, and if there had been a day, seven years ago, when the sun came out for an hour and showed its face to the stunned world, they could not recall. Sometimes, at night, she heard them stir, in remembrance, and she knew they were dreaming and remembering gold or a yellow crayon or a coin large enough to buy the world with. She knew they thought they remembered a warmness, like a blushing in the face, in the body, in the arms and legs and trembling hands. But then they always awoke to the tatting drum, the endless shaking down of clear bead necklaces upon the roof, the walk, the gardens, the forests, and their dreams were gone.

All day yesterday they had read in class about the sun. About how like a lemon it was, and how hot. And they had written small stories or essays or poems about it:

I think the sun is a flower,
That blooms for just one hour.

That was Margot's poem, read in a quiet voice in the still classroom while the rain was falling outside.

"Aw, you didn't write that!" protested one of the boys.

"I did," said Margot. "I *did*."

"William!" said the teacher.

But that was yesterday. Now the rain was slackening, and the children were crushed in the great thick windows.

"Where's teacher?"

"She'll be back."

"She'd better hurry; we'll miss it!"

They turned on themselves, like a feverish wheel, all tumbling spokes.

Margot stood alone. She was a very frail girl, who looked as if she had been lost in the rain for years and the rain had washed out the blue from her eyes and the red from her mouth and the yellow from her hair. She was an old photograph dusted from an album, whitened away, and if she spoke at all her voice would be a ghost. Now she stood, separate, staring at the rain and the loud wet world beyond the huge glass.

"What're *you* looking at?" said William.

Margot said nothing.

"Speak when you're spoken to." He gave her a shove. But she did not move; rather she let herself be moved only by him and nothing else.

They edged away from her; they would not look at her. She felt them go away. And this was because she would play no games with them in the echoing tunnels of the underground city. If they tagged her and ran, she stood blinking after them and did not follow. When the class sang songs about happiness and life and games, her lips barely moved. Only when they sang about the sun and the summer did her lips move as she watched the drenched windows.

And then, of course, the biggest crime of all was that she had come here only five years ago from Earth, and she remembered the sun and the way the sun was and the sky was when she was four in Ohio. And they, they had been on Venus all their lives, and they had been only two years old when last the sun came out and had long since forgotten the color and heat of it and the way it really was. But Margot remembered.

"It's like a penny," she said once, eyes closed.

"No, it's not!" the children cried.

"It's like a fire," she said, "in the stove."

"You're lying, you don't remember!" cried the children.

But she remembered and stood quietly apart from all of them and watched the patterning windows. And once, a month ago, she had refused to shower in the school shower rooms, had clutched her hands to her ears and over her head, screaming the water mustn't touch her head. So after that, dimly, dimly, she sensed it, she was different, and they knew her difference and kept away.

There was talk that her father and mother were taking her back to Earth next year; it seemed vital to her that they do so, though it would mean the loss of thousands of dollars to her family. And so, the children hated her for all these reasons of big and little consequence. They hated her pale snow face, her waiting silence, her thinness, and her possible future.

"Get away!" The boy gave her another push. "What're you waiting for?"

Then, for the first time, she turned and looked at him. And what she was waiting for was in her eyes.

"Well, don't wait around here!" cried the boy savagely. "You won't see nothing!"

Her lips moved.

"Nothing!" he cried. "It was all a joke, wasn't it?" He turned to the other children. "Nothing's happening today. *Is* it?"

They all blinked at him and then, understanding, laughed and shook their heads. "Nothing, nothing!"

"Oh, but," Margot whispered, her eyes helpless. "But this is the day, the scientists predict, they say, they *know*, the sun . . . "

"All a joke!" said the boy, and seized her roughly. "Hey, everyone, let's put her in a closet before teacher comes!"

"No," said Margot, falling back.

They surged about her, caught her up, and bore her, protesting, and then pleading, and then crying, back into a tunnel, a room, a closet, where they slammed and locked the door. They stood looking at the door and saw it tremble from her beating and throwing herself against it. They heard her muffled cries. Then, smiling, they turned and went out and back down the tunnel, just as the teacher arrived.

"Ready, children?" She glanced at her watch.

"Yes!" said everyone.

"Are we all here?"

"Yes!"

The rain slackened still more.

They crowded to the huge door.

The rain stopped.

It was as if, in the midst of a film concerning an avalanche, a tornado, a hurricane, a volcanic eruption, something had, first, gone wrong with the sound apparatus, thus muffling and finally cutting off all noise, all of the blasts and repercussions and thunders, and then, second, ripped the film from the projector and inserted in its place a peaceful tropical slide which did not move or tremor. The world ground to a standstill. The silence was so immense and unbelievable that you felt your ears had been stuffed or you had lost your hearing altogether. The children put their hands to their ears. They stood apart. The door slid back, and the smell of the silent, waiting world came in to them.

The sun came out.

It was the color of flaming bronze, and it was very large. And the sky around it was a blazing blue tile color.

And the jungle burned with sunlight as the children, released from their spell, rushed out, yelling, into the springtime.

"Now, don't go too far," called the teacher after them. "You've only two hours, you know. You wouldn't want to get caught out!"

But they were running and turning their faces up to the sky and feeling the sun on their cheeks like a warm iron; they were taking off their jackets and letting the sun burn their arms.

"Oh, it's better than the sun lamps, isn't it?"

"Much, much better!"

They stopped running and stood in the great jungle that covered Venus, that grew and never stopped growing, tumultuously, even as you watched it. It was a nest of octopi, clustering up great arms of fleshlike weed, wavering, flowering in this brief spring. It was the color of rubber and ash, this jungle, from the many years without sun. It was the color of stones and white cheeses and ink, and it was the color of the moon.

The children lay out, laughing, on the jungle mattress, and heard it sigh and squeak under them, resilient and alive. They ran among the trees, they slipped and fell, they pushed each other, they played hide-and-seek and tag, but most of all they squinted at the sun until tears ran down their faces; they put their hands up to that yellowness and that amazing blueness, and they breathed of the fresh, fresh air and listened and listened to the silence which suspended them in a blessed sea of no sound and no motion. They looked at everything and savored everything. Then, wildly, like animals escaped from their caves, they ran and ran in shouting circles. They ran for an hour and did not stop running.

And then—

In the midst of their running one of the girls wailed.

Everyone stopped.

The girl, standing in the open, held out her hand.

"Oh, look, look," she said, trembling.

They came slowly to look at her opened palm.

In the center of it, cupped and huge, was a single raindrop.

She began to cry, looking at it.

They glanced quietly at the sky.

"Oh. Oh."

A few cold drops fell on their noses and their cheeks and their mouths. The sun faded behind a stir of mist. A wind blew cool around them. They turned and started to walk back toward the underground house, their hands at their sides, their smiles vanishing away.

A boom of thunder startled them and, like leaves before a new hurricane, they tumbled upon each other and ran. Lightning struck ten miles away, five miles away, a mile, a half mile. The sky darkened into midnight in a flash.

They stood in the doorway of the underground for a moment until it was raining hard. Then they closed the door and heard the gigantic sound of the rain falling in tons and avalanches, everywhere and forever.

"Will it be seven more years?"

"Yes. Seven."

Then one of them gave a little cry.

"Margot!"

"What?"

"She's still in the closet where we locked her."

"Margot."

They stood as if someone had driven them, like so many stakes, into the floor. They looked at each other and then looked away. They glanced out at the world that was raining now and raining and raining steadily. They could not meet each other's glances. Their faces were solemn and pale. They looked at their hands and feet, their faces down.

"Margot."

One of the girls said, "Well . . . ?"

No one moved.

"Go on," whispered the girl.

They walked slowly down the hall in the sound of cold rain. They turned through the doorway to the room in the sound of the storm and thunder, lightning on their faces, blue and terrible. They walked over to the closet door slowly and stood by it.

Behind the closet door was only silence.

They unlocked the door, even more slowly, and let Margot out.

"Little you know what this rose has cost."

BEAUTY AND THE BEAST

Madame de Villeneuve

Once upon a time, in a far-off country, there lived a merchant who had been so fortunate in all his undertakings that he was enormously rich. As he had six sons and six daughters, however, who were accustomed to having everything they fancied, he did not find he had a penny too much. But misfortunes befell them. One day their house caught fire and speedily burned to the ground, with all the splendid furniture, books, pictures, gold, silver, and precious goods it contained. The father suddenly lost every ship he had upon the sea, either by dint of pirates, shipwreck, or fire. Then he heard that his clerks in distant countries, whom he had trusted entirely, had proved unfaithful. And at last from great wealth he fell into the direst poverty.

All that he had left was a little house in a desolate place at least a hundred leagues from the town, and to this he was forced to retreat. His children were in despair at the idea of leading such a different life. The daughters at first hoped their friends, who had been so numerous while they were rich, would insist on their staying in their houses, but they soon found they were left alone. Their former friends even attributed their misfortunes to their own extravagance and showed no intention of offering them any help.

So nothing was left for them but to take their departure to the cottage, which stood in the midst of a dark forest and seemed to be the most dismal place on the face of the earth. As they were too poor to have any servants, the girls had to work hard, and the sons, for their part, cultivated the fields to earn their living. Roughly clothed and living in the simplest way, the girls regretted unceasingly the luxuries and amusements of their former life. Only the youngest daughter tried to be brave and cheerful.

She had been as sad as anyone when misfortune first overtook her father, but soon recovering her natural gaiety, she set to work to make the best of things, to amuse her father and brothers as well as she could, and to persuade her sisters to join her in dancing and singing. But they would do nothing of the sort, and because she was not as doleful as themselves, they declared this miserable life was all she was fit for. But she was really far prettier and cleverer than they were. Indeed, she was so lovely she was always called Beauty.

After two years, when they were all beginning to get used to their new life, their father received news that one of his ships, which he had believed lost, had come safely into port with a rich cargo. All the sons and daughters at once thought that their poverty was at an end and wanted to set out directly for the town; but their father, who was more prudent, begged them to wait a little, and though it was harvest time, and he could ill be spared, determined to go himself to make inquiries.

Only the youngest daughter had any doubt but that they would soon again be as rich as they were before. They all loaded their father with commissions for jewels and dresses which it would have taken a fortune to buy; only Beauty, feeling sure that it was of no use, did not ask for anything. Her father, noticing her silence, said: "And what shall I bring for you, Beauty?"

"The only thing I wish for is to see you come home safely," she answered.

But this reply vexed her sisters, who fancied she was blaming them for having asked for such costly things. Her father, however, was pleased, but as he thought that at her age she certainly ought to like pretty presents, he told her to choose something.

"Well, dear Father," she said, "as you insist upon it, I beg that you will bring me a rose. I have not seen one since we came here, and I love them so much."

The merchant reached town as quickly as possible, only to find that his former companions, believing him to be dead, had divided his cargo between them. After six months of trouble and expense, he found himself as poor as when he started on his journey. To make matters worse, he was obliged to return in the most terrible weather. By the time he was within a few leagues of his home, he was almost exhausted with cold and fatigue. Though he knew it would take some hours to get through the forest, he resolved to go on. But night overtook him, and the deep snow and bitter frost made it impossible for his horse to carry him any farther.

Not a house was to be seen. The only shelter he could get was the hollow trunk of a great tree, and there he crouched all the night, which seemed to him the longest he had ever known. The howling of the wolves kept him awake, and when at last day broke, the falling snow had covered up every path, and he did not know which way to turn.

At length he made out some sort of path, but it was so rough and slippery that he fell down more than once. Presently it led him into an avenue of trees which ended in a splendid castle. It seemed to the merchant very strange that no snow had fallen in the avenue of orange trees, covered with flowers and fruit. When he reached the first court of the castle, he saw before him a flight of agate steps. He went up them and passed through several splendidly furnished rooms.

The pleasant warmth of the air revived him, and he felt very hungry; but there seemed to be nobody in all this vast and splendid palace. Deep silence reigned everywhere, and at last, tired of roaming through empty rooms and galleries, he stopped in a room smaller than the rest, where a clear fire was burning, and a couch was drawn up cosily before it. Thinking this must be prepared for someone who was expected, he sat down to wait till he should come and very soon fell into a sweet sleep.

When his extreme hunger wakened him after several hours, he was still alone; but a little table, with a good dinner on it, had been drawn up close to him. He lost no time in beginning his meal, hoping he might soon thank his considerate host, whoever it might be. But no one appeared, and even after another long sleep, from which he awoke completely refreshed, there was no sign of anybody, though a fresh meal of dainty cakes and fruit was prepared upon the little table at his elbow.

Because he was naturally timid, the silence began to terrify him, and he resolved to search once more through all the rooms; but it was of no use; there was no sign of life in the palace! He wondered what he should do. To amuse himself, he began pretending that all the treasures he saw were his own and considering how he would divide them among his children. Then he went down into the garden, and though it was winter everywhere else, here the sun shone, the birds sang, the flowers bloomed, and the air was soft and sweet. The merchant, in ecstasies with all he saw and heard, said to himself:

"All this must be meant for me. I will go this minute and bring my children to share all these delights."

In spite of being so cold and weary when he reached the castle, he had taken his horse to the stable and fed it. Now he thought he would saddle it for his homeward journey, and he turned down the path which led to the stable. This path had a hedge of roses on each side of it, and the merchant thought he had never seen such exquisite flowers. They reminded him of his promise to Beauty, and he stopped and had just gathered one to take to her when he was startled by a strange noise behind him. Turning round, he saw a frightful Beast, which seemed to be very angry and said in a terrible voice:

"Who told you you might gather my roses? Was it not enough that I sheltered you in my palace and was kind to you? This is the way you show your gratitude, by stealing my flowers! But your insolence shall not go unpunished."

The merchant, terrified by these furious words, dropped the fatal rose and, throwing himself on his knees, cried, "Pardon me, noble sir. I am truly grateful for your hospitality, which was so magnificent I could not imagine you would be offended by my taking such a little thing as a rose."

But the Beast's anger was not lessened by his speech. "You are very ready with excuses and flattery," he cried. "But that will not save you from the death you deserve."

Alas, thought the merchant, if my daughter Beauty could only know into what danger her rose has brought me! And in despair he began to tell the Beast all his misfortunes and the reason of his journey, not forgetting to mention Beauty's request.

"A king's ransom would hardly have procured all that my other daughters asked for," he said. "But I thought I might at least take Beauty her rose. I beg you to forgive me, for you see I meant no harm."

The Beast said, in a less furious tone, "I will forgive you on one condition—that you will give me one of your daughters."

"Ah," cried the merchant, "if I were cruel enough to buy my own life at the expense of one of my children's, what excuse could I invent to bring her here?"

"None," answered the Beast. "If she comes at all, she must come willingly. On no other condition will I have her. See if any one of them is courageous enough and loves you enough to come and save your life. You seem to be an honest man, so I will trust you to go home. I give you a month to see if any of your daughters will come back with you and stay here, to let you go free. If none of them is willing, you must come alone, after bidding them goodbye forever, for then you will belong to me. And do not imagine that you can hide from me, for if you fail to keep your word, I will come and fetch you!" added the Beast grimly.

The merchant accepted this proposal though he did not really think that any of his daughters would be persuaded to come. He promised to return at the time appointed, and then, anxious to escape from the presence of the Beast, he asked permission to set off at once. But the Beast answered that he could not go until the next day.

"Then you will find a horse ready for you," he said. "Now go and eat your supper and await my orders."

The poor merchant, more dead than alive, went back to his room, where the most delicious supper was already served on the little table drawn up before a blazing fire. But he was too terrified to eat and only tasted a few of the dishes, for fear the Beast should be angry if he did not obey his orders. When he had finished, he heard a great noise in the next room, which he knew meant that the Beast was coming. As he could do nothing to escape his visit, the only thing that remained was to seem as little afraid as possible; so when the Beast appeared and asked roughly if he had supped well, the merchant answered humbly that he had, thanks to his host's kindness. Then the Beast warned him to remember their agreement and to prepare his daughter exactly for what she had to expect.

"Do not get up tomorrow," he added, "until you see the sun and hear a golden bell ring. Then you will find your breakfast waiting for you, and the horse you are to ride will be ready in the courtyard. He will also bring you back again when you come with your daughter a month hence. Farewell. Take a rose to Beauty, and remember your promise!"

The merchant lay down until the sun rose. Then, after breakfast, he went to gather Beauty's rose and mounted his horse, which carried him off so swiftly that in an instant he had lost sight of the palace. He was still wrapped in gloomy thoughts when the horse stopped before the door of his cottage.

His sons and daughters, who had been uneasy at his long absence, rushed to meet him, eager to know the result of his journey which, seeing him mounted upon a splendid horse and wrapped in a rich mantle, they supposed to be favorable. But he hid the truth from them at first, only saying sadly to Beauty as he gave her the rose:

"Here is what you asked me to bring you. Little you know what it has cost."

But this excited their curiosity so greatly that presently he told them his adventures from beginning to end, and then they were all very unhappy. The girls lamented loudly over their lost hopes, and the sons declared their father should not return to the terrible castle, and began to make plans for killing the Beast if it should come to fetch him. But he reminded them he had promised to go back. Then the girls were very angry with Beauty and said it was all her fault. If she had asked for something sensible, this would never have happened.

Poor Beauty, much distressed, said to them, "I have indeed caused this misfortune, but who could have guessed that to ask for a rose in the middle of summer would cause so much misery? But as I did the mischief, it is only just that I should suffer for it. I will therefore go back with my father to keep his promise."

At first nobody would hear of it. Her father and brothers, who loved her dearly, declared nothing should make them let her go. But Beauty was firm. As the time drew near, she divided her little possessions between her sisters and said goodbye to everything she loved. When the fatal day came, she encouraged and cheered her father as they mounted together the horse which had brought him back. It seemed to fly rather than gallop, but so smoothly that Beauty was not frightened. Indeed, she would have enjoyed the journey, if she had not feared what might happen at the end of it. Her father still tried to persuade her to go back, but in vain.

While they were talking, the night fell. Then, to their great surprise, wonderful colored lights began to shine in all directions, and splendid fireworks blazed out before them; all the forest was illuminated. They even felt pleasantly warm, though it had been bitterly cold before. They reached the avenue of orange trees and saw that the palace was brilliantly lighted from roof to ground, and music sounded softly from the courtyard.

"The Beast must be very hungry," said Beauty, trying to laugh, "if he makes all this rejoicing over the arrival of his prey." But in spite of her anxiety, she admired all the wonderful things she saw.

When they had dismounted, her father led her to the little room he had been in before. Here they found a splendid fire burning and the table daintily spread with a delicious supper.

The merchant knew that this was meant for them, and Beauty, who was less frightened now that she had passed through so many rooms and seen nothing of the Beast, was quite willing to begin, for her long ride had made her very hungry. But they had hardly finished their meal, when the noise of the Beast's footsteps was heard approaching, and Beauty clung to her father in terror, which became all the greater when she saw how frightened he was. But when the Beast really appeared, though she trembled at the sight of him, she made a great effort to hide her horror and saluted him respectfully.

This evidently pleased the Beast. After looking at her he said, in a tone that might have struck terror into the boldest heart, though he did not seem to be angry:

"Good evening, old man. Good evening, Beauty."

The merchant was too terrified to reply, but Beauty answered sweetly, "Good evening, Beast."

"Have you come willingly?" asked the Beast. "Will you be content to stay here when your father goes away?"

Beauty answered bravely that she was quite prepared to stay.

"I am pleased with you," said the Beast. "As you have come of your own accord, you may remain. As for you, old man," he added, turning to the merchant, "at sunrise tomorrow take your departure. When the bell rings, get up quickly and eat your breakfast, and you will find the same horse waiting to take you home. But remember that you must never expect to see my palace again."

Then turning to Beauty, he said, "Take your father into the next room and help him choose gifts for your brothers and sisters. You will find two traveling trunks there; fill them as full as you can. It is only just that you should send them something very precious as a remembrance."

Then he went away, after saying, "Goodbye, Beauty; goodbye, old man." Beauty was beginning to think with great dismay of her father's departure, but she was afraid to disobey the Beast's orders. They went into the next room, which had shelves and cupboards all round it. They were greatly surprised at the riches it contained. There were splendid dresses fit for a queen, with all the ornaments to be worn with them, and when Beauty opened the cupboards, she was dazzled by the gorgeous jewels lying in heaps upon every shelf. After choosing a vast quantity, which she divided between her sisters—for she had made a heap of the wonderful dresses for each of them—she opened the last chest, which was full of gold.

"I think, Father," she said, "that, as the gold will be more useful to you, we had better take out the other things again, and fill the trunks with it."

So they did this, but the more they put in, the more room there seemed to be, and at last they put back all the jewels and dresses they had taken out, and Beauty even added as many more of the jewels as she could carry at once. Even then the trunks were not too full, but they were so heavy an elephant could not have carried them!

"The Beast was mocking us!" cried the merchant. "He pretended to give us all these things, knowing that I could not carry them away."

"Let us wait and see," answered Beauty. "I cannot believe he meant to deceive us. All we can do is to fasten them up and have them ready."

So they did this and returned to the little room where, to their astonishment, they found breakfast ready. The merchant ate his with a good appetite, as the Beast's generosity made him believe he might perhaps venture to come back soon and see Beauty. But she felt sure her father was leaving her forever, so she was very sad when the bell rang sharply for the second time and warned them that the time was come for them to part.

They went down into the courtyard, where two horses were waiting, one loaded with the two trunks, the other for him to ride. They were pawing the ground in their impatience to start, and the merchant bade Beauty a hasty farewell. As soon as he was mounted, he went off at such a pace she lost sight of him in an instant. Then Beauty began to cry and wandered sadly back to her own room. But she soon found she was very sleepy, and as she had nothing better to do, she lay down and instantly fell asleep. And then she dreamed she was walking by a brook bordered with trees and lamenting her sad fate, when a young prince, handsomer than anyone she had ever seen, and with a voice that went straight to her heart, came and said to her:

"Ah, Beauty, you are not so unfortunate as you suppose. Here you will be rewarded for all you have suffered elsewhere. Your every wish shall be gratified. Only try to find me out, no matter how I may be disguised, for I love you dearly, and in making me happy, you will find your own happiness. Be as truehearted as you are beautiful, and we shall have nothing left to wish for."

"What can I do, Prince, to make you happy?" said Beauty.

"Only be grateful," he answered, "and do not trust too much to your eyes. Above all, do not desert me until you have saved me from my cruel misery."

After this she thought she found herself in a room with a stately and beautiful lady, who said to her, "Dear Beauty, try not to regret all you have left behind you;

you are destined for a better fate. Only do not let yourself be deceived by appearances."

Beauty found her dreams so interesting that she was in no hurry to awake, but presently the clock roused her by calling her name softly twelve times. Then she rose and found her dressing table set out with everything she could possibly want, and when her toilet was finished, she found dinner waiting in the room next to hers. But dinner does not take very long when one is alone, and very soon she sat down cozily in the corner of a sofa and began to think about the charming prince she had seen in her dream.

"He said I could make him happy," said Beauty to herself. "It seems, then, that this horrible Beast keeps him a prisoner. How can I set him free? I wonder why they both told me not to trust to appearances? But after all, it was only a dream, so why should I trouble myself about it? I had better find something to do to amuse myself."

So she began to explore some of the many rooms of the palace. The first she entered was lined with mirrors. Beauty saw herself reflected on every side and thought she had never seen such a charming room. Then a bracelet which was hanging from a chandelier caught her eye, and on taking it down, she was greatly surprised to find that it held a portrait of her unknown admirer, just as she had seen him in her dream. With great delight she slipped the bracelet on her arm and went on into a gallery of pictures, where she soon found a portrait of the same handsome prince, as large as life, and so well painted that as she studied it, he seemed to smile kindly at her.

Tearing herself away from the portrait at last, she passed into a room which contained every musical instrument under the sun, and here she amused herself for a long while in trying them and singing until she was tired. The next room was a library, and she saw everything she had ever wanted to read as well as everything she had read. By this time it was growing dusk, and wax candles in diamond and ruby candlesticks lit themselves in every room.

Beauty found her supper served just at the time she preferred to have it, but she did not see anyone or hear a sound. Though her father had warned her she would be alone, she began to find it rather dull.

Presently she heard the Beast coming and wondered tremblingly if he meant to eat her now. However, he did not seem at all ferocious and only said gruffly:

"Good evening, Beauty."

She answered cheerfully and managed to conceal her terror. The Beast asked how she had been amusing herself, and she told him all the rooms she had seen. Then he asked if she thought she could be happy in his palace, and Beauty answered that everything was so beautiful she would be very hard to please if she could not be happy. After about an hour's talk, Beauty began to think the Beast was not nearly so terrible as she had supposed at first. Then he rose to leave her and said in his gruff voice:

"Do you love me, Beauty? Will you marry me?"

"Oh, what shall I say?" cried Beauty, for she was afraid to make the Beast angry by refusing.

"Say yes or no without fear," he replied.

"Oh, no, Beast," said Beauty hastily.

"Since you will not, good night, Beauty," he said.

And she answered, "Good night, Beast," very glad to find her refusal had not provoked him. After he was gone, she was very soon in bed and dreaming of her unknown prince.

She thought he came and said, "Ah, Beauty! Why are you so unkind to me? I fear I am fated to be unhappy for many a long day still."

Then her dreams changed, but the charming prince figured in them all. When morning came, her first thought was to look at the portrait and see if it was really like him, and she found it certainly was.

She decided to amuse herself in the garden, for the sun shone, and all the fountains were playing. She was astonished to find that every place was familiar to her, and presently she came to the very brook and the myrtle trees where she had first met the prince in her dream. That made her think more than ever he must be kept a prisoner by the Beast.

When she was tired, she went back to the palace and found a new room full of materials for every kind of work—ribbons to make into bows and silks to work into flowers. There was an aviary full of rare birds, which were so tame they flew to Beauty as soon as they saw her and perched upon her shoulders and her head.

"Pretty little creatures," she said, "how I wish your cage was nearer my room that I might often hear you sing!" So saying, she opened a door and found to her delight that it led into her own room, though she had thought it was on the other side of the palace.

There were more birds in a room farther on, parrots and cockatoos that could talk, and they greeted Beauty by name. Indeed, she found them so entertaining that she took one or two back to her room, and they talked to her while she was at supper. The Beast paid her his usual visit and asked the same questions as before, and then with a gruff good night he took his departure, and Beauty went to bed to dream of her mysterious prince.

The days passed swiftly in different amusements, and after a while Beauty found another strange thing in the palace, which often pleased her when she was tired of being alone. There was one room which she had not noticed particularly; it was empty, except that under each of the windows stood a very comfortable chair. The first time she had looked out of the window, it seemed a black curtain prevented her from seeing anything outside. But the second time she went into the room, happening to be tired, she sat down in one of the chairs, when instantly the curtain was rolled aside, and a most amusing pantomime was acted before her. There were dances and colored lights, music and pretty dresses, and it was all so gay that Beauty was in ecstasies. After that she tried the other seven windows in turn, and there was some new and surprising entertainment to be seen from each of them, so Beauty never could feel lonely any more. Every evening after supper, the Beast came to see her and always before saying good night asked her in his terrible voice:

"Beauty, will you marry me?"

And it seemed to Beauty, now she understood him better, that when she said, "No, Beast," he went away quite sad. Her happy dreams of the handsome young prince soon made her forget the poor Beast, and the only thing that disturbed her was being told to distrust appearances, to let her heart guide her, and not her eyes. Consider as she would, she could not understand.

So everything went on for a long time, until at last, happy as she was, Beauty began to long for the sight of her father and her brothers and sisters. One night, seeing her look very sad, the Beast asked her what was the matter. Beauty had quite ceased to be afraid of him. Now she knew he was really gentle in spite of his ferocious looks and his dreadful voice. So she answered that she wished to see her home once more. Upon hearing this, the Beast seemed sadly distressed and cried miserably:

"Ah, Beauty, have you the heart to desert an unhappy Beast like this? What more do you want to make you happy? Is it because you hate me that you want to escape?"

"No, dear Beast," answered Beauty softly, "I do not hate you, and I should be very sorry never to see you any more, but I long to see my father again. Only let me go for two months, and I promise to come back to you and stay for the rest of my life."

The Beast, who had been sighing dolefully while she spoke, now replied, "I cannot refuse you anything you ask, even though it should cost me my life. Take the four boxes you will find in the room next to your own and fill them with everything you wish to take with you. But remember your promise and come back when the two months are over, or you may have cause to repent it; for if you do not come in good time you will find your faithful Beast dead. You will not need any chariot to bring you back. Only say goodbye to all your brothers and sisters the night before you come away and, when you have gone to bed, turn this ring round upon your finger, and say firmly, 'I wish to go back to my palace and see my Beast again.' Good night, Beauty. Fear nothing, sleep peacefully, and before long you shall see your father once more."

As soon as Beauty was alone, she hastened to fill the boxes with all the rare and precious things she saw about her, and only when she was tired of heaping things into them did they seem to be full. Then she went to bed but could hardly sleep for joy. When at last she began to dream of her beloved prince, she was grieved to see him stretched upon a grassy bank, sad and weary, and hardly like himself.

"What is the matter?" she cried.

But he looked at her reproachfully and said, "How can you ask me, cruel one? Are you not leaving me to my death perhaps?"

"Ah, don't be so sorrowful!" cried Beauty. "I am only going to assure my father that I am safe and happy. I have promised the Beast faithfully I will come back, and he would die of grief if I did not keep my word!"

"What would that matter to you?" asked the prince. "Surely you would not care?"

"Indeed I should be ungrateful if I did not care for such a kind Beast," cried Beauty indignantly. "I would die to save him from pain. I assure you it is not his fault he is so ugly."

Just then a strange sound woke her—someone was speaking not very far away; and opening her eyes she found herself in a room she had never seen before, which was certainly not as splendid as those she had seen in the Beast's palace. Where could she be? She rose and dressed hastily and then saw that the boxes she had packed the night before were all in the room. Suddenly she heard her father's voice and rushed out to greet him joyfully.

Her brothers and sisters were astonished at her appearance, for they had never expected to see her again. There was no end to the questions they asked her. She had also much to hear about what had happened to them while she was away and of her father's journey home. But when they heard that she had only come to be with them for a short time and then must go back to the Beast's palace forever, they lamented loudly. Then Beauty asked her father what he thought her strange dreams meant and why the prince constantly begged her not to trust to appearances. After much consideration he answered:

"You tell me yourself that the Beast, frightful as he is, loves you dearly and deserves your love and gratitude for his gentleness and kindness. I think the prince must mean you to understand you ought to reward him by doing as he wishes, in spite of his ugliness."

Beauty could not help seeing that this seemed probable; still, when she thought of her dear prince who was so handsome, she did not feel at all inclined to marry the Beast. At any rate, for two months she need not decide but could enjoy herself with her sisters. But though they were rich now and lived in a town again and had plenty of acquaintances, Beauty found that nothing amused her very much. She often thought of the palace, where she was so happy, especially as at home she never once dreamed of her dear prince, and she felt quite sad without him.

Then her sisters seemed quite used to being without her and even found her rather in the way, so she would not have been sorry when the two months were over, but for her father and brothers, who begged her to stay and seemed so grieved at the thought of her departure that she had not the courage to say goodbye to them. Every day when she rose she meant to say it at night, and when night came she put it off again, until at last she had a dismal dream which helped her to make up her mind.

She thought she was wandering in a lonely path in the palace gardens, when she heard groans that seemed to come from some bushes hiding the entrance of a cave. Running quickly to see what could be the matter, she found the Beast stretched out upon his side, apparently dying. He reproached her faintly with being the cause of his distress, and at the same moment a stately lady appeared and said very gravely:

"Ah, Beauty, see what happens when people do not keep their promises! If you had delayed one day more, you would have found him dead."

Beauty was so terrified by this dream that the next morning she announced her intention of going back at once. That very evening she said goodbye to her father and her brothers and sisters, and as soon as she was in bed she turned her ring round upon her finger and said firmly:

"I wish to go back to my palace and see my Beast again."

Then she fell asleep instantly and only woke up to hear the clock saying, "Beauty, Beauty," twelve times in its musical voice, which told her she was really in the palace once more. Everything was just as before, and her birds were so glad to see her, but Beauty thought she had never known such a long day. She was so anxious to see the Beast again that she felt as if suppertime would never come.

But when it came, no Beast appeared. After listening and waiting for a long time, she ran down into the garden to search for him. Up and down the paths and avenues ran poor Beauty, calling him. No one answered, and not a trace of him could she find. At last, quite tired, she stopped for a minute's rest and saw that she was standing opposite the shady path she had seen in her dream. She rushed down it and, sure enough, there was the cave, and in it lay the Beast—asleep, so Beauty thought. Quite glad to have found him, she ran up and stroked his head, but to her horror he did not move or open his eyes.

"Oh, he is dead, and it is all my fault!" cried Beauty, crying bitterly.

But then, looking at him again, she fancied he still breathed. Hastily fetching some water from the nearest fountain, she sprinkled it over his face, and to her great delight he began to revive.

"Oh, Beast, how you frightened me!" she cried. "I never knew how much I loved you until just now, when I feared I was too late to save your life."

"Can you really love such an ugly creature as I am?" asked the Beast faintly. "Ah, Beauty, you came only just in time. I was dying because I thought you had forgotten your promise. But go back now and rest; I shall see you again by and by."

Beauty, who had half expected he would be angry with her, was reassured by his gentle voice and went back to the palace, where supper was awaiting her. And afterward the Beast came in as usual and talked about the time she had spent with her father, asking if she had enjoyed herself and if they had all been glad to see her.

Beauty quite enjoyed telling him all that had happened to her. When at last the time came for him to go, he asked, as he had so often asked before:

"Beauty, will you marry me?"

She answered softly, "Yes, dear Beast."

As she spoke a blaze of light sprang up before the windows of the palace; fireworks crackled and guns banged, and across the avenue of orange trees, in letters all made of fireflies, was written: *Long live the prince and his bride.*

Turning to ask the Beast what it could all mean, Beauty found he had disappeared, and in his place stood her long-loved prince! At the same moment the wheels of a chariot were heard upon the terrace, and two ladies entered the room. One of them Beauty recognized as the stately lady she had seen in her dreams; the other was so queenly that Beauty hardly knew which to greet first. But the one she already knew said to her companion:

"Well, Queen, this is Beauty, who has had the courage to rescue your son from the terrible enchantment. They love each other, and only your consent to their marriage is wanting to make them perfectly happy."

"I consent with all my heart," cried the queen. "How can I ever thank you enough, charming girl, for having restored my dear son to his natural form?" And then she tenderly embraced Beauty and the prince, who had meanwhile been greeting the fairy and receiving her congratulations.

"Now," said the fairy to Beauty, "I suppose you would like me to send for all your brothers and sisters to dance at your wedding?"

And so she did, and the marriage was celebrated the very next day with the utmost splendor, and Beauty and the prince lived happily ever after.

ACKNOWLEDGMENTS

All possible care has been taken to trace ownership and secure permission for each selection in this series. The Great Books Foundation wishes to thank the following authors, publishers, and representatives for permission to reprint copyrighted material:

Thank You, M'am, from THE LANGSTON HUGHES READER. Copyright © 1958 by Langston Hughes, renewed 1986 by George Houston Bass. Reprinted by permission of Harold Ober Associates, Inc.

THE GOLD COIN, by Alma Flor Ada, translated by Bernice Randall. Copyright © 1991 by Alma Flor Ada. Reprinted by permission of Atheneum Books for Young Readers, an imprint of Simon & Schuster Children's Publishing Division.

Tuesday of the Other June, by Norma Fox Mazer, from SHORT TAKES: A SHORT STORY COLLECTION FOR YOUNG READERS, edited by Elizabeth Segel. Copyright © 1986 by Lothrop, Lee & Shepard. Reprinted by permission of the author.

Prot and Krot, from THE AMBER MOUNTAIN AND OTHER FOLK STORIES, by Agnes Szudek. Copyright © 1976 by Agnes Szudek. Reprinted by permission of the author.

CHIN YU MIN AND THE GINGER CAT, by Jennifer Armstrong. Copyright © 1993 by Jennifer Armstrong. Reprinted by permission of Random House Children's Books, a division of Random House, Inc. All rights reserved.

The Nightingale, from HANS CHRISTIAN ANDERSEN: HIS CLASSIC FAIRY TALES, translated by Erik Haugaard. Translation copyright © 1974 by Erik Christian Haugaard. Reprinted by permission of Doubleday, a division of Random House, Inc.

Fresh, from WHAT THE NEIGHBOURS DID AND OTHER STORIES, by Philippa Pearce. Copyright © 1959, 1967, 1969, 1972 by Philippa Pearce. Reprinted by permission of Laura Cecil Literary Agency and the author.

Thunder, Elephant, and Dorobo, from TALES TOLD NEAR A CROCODILE, by Humphrey Harman. Copyright © 1962 by Humphrey Harman. Published by Hutchinson. Reprinted by permission of the Random House Group, Ltd.

All Summer in a Day, from THE STORIES OF RAY BRADBURY. Originally appeared in the *Magazine of Fantasy and Science Fiction.* Copyright © 1954, 1982 by Ray Bradbury. Reprinted by permission of Don Congdon Associates, Inc.

ILLUSTRATION CREDITS

Carll Cneut prepared the illustration for *Chin Yu Min and the Ginger Cat.*

Brock Cole prepared the illustration for *Prot and Krot.*

David Cunningham prepared the illustration for *Thank You, M'am.*

Tom Feelings prepared the illustration for *Thunder, Elephant, and Dorobo.* Reprinted by permission of the Estate of Tom Feelings.

Marilee Heyer prepared the illustration for *The Nightingale.*

Ron Himler prepared the illustration for *Tuesday of the Other June.*

Paul Hoffman prepared the illustration for *Beauty and the Beast.*

Rosalind Kaye prepared the illustration for *The Gold Coin.*

Emily McCully prepared the illustration for *Fresh.*

Omar Rayyan prepared the illustration for *All Summer in a Day.*

Cover art by Louise Brierley. Copyright © 2006 by Louise Brierley.

Text and cover design by William Seabright & Associates.

Interior design by Think Design Group.